Help a Kid in Love

"Tell the World You Love Someone and Mend a Broken Heart"

(A True Story in the Making)

Copyleft ⊗ 2006 by Christopher Glen Miller. Some rights reserved.

Published by Chris Miller, Help a Kid in Love. Omaha, Nebraska, USA

Chris Miller
4837 Farnam St.
Omaha, NE 68132
(402) 432-3495
Email: chris@helpakidinlove.com
Web: http://www.HelpaKidinLove.com

The hardest part about publishing and marketing your first book is getting word out about the book and making people aware of the book. For that reason, I do not know why so many other first time published authors do not ask for help in that area on the first page. If I sincerely intend to tell the *entire* world who I love in one lifetime, I have no time to mess around with playing copyright police. The goal of telling the entire world one message in one lifetime means much more to me than sucking every royalty penny I can out of a copyright.

I encourage you to use any material from this book for any reason with good intentions other than for your own financial gain. If I wrote something that you want to share with others, please share that information with them at your best judgment. As a copylefted book, you have the right to share, modify, and distribute this book to whomever you wish; however, you have no rights to copyright any duplicate or modification from the original document, and you have no rights to copyright the original document itself.

One favor I ask of you, is to contact me via e-mail (chris@helpakidinlove.com), or snail mail (address listed above) if you would like distribute, share, or modify my book. Without my consent, it would be highly unethical for you to use information from this book for selfish interests. With good intentions, I would be thrilled to see you helping me tell other people what I have written. After all, the entire world is going to find out about this book sooner or later, and frankly, I am not concerned with who tells who first about this book, just contact me before you plagiarize.

Miller, Christopher Glen
    Help a Kid in Love: Tell the World You Love Someone
                   and Mend a Broken Heart – 1st ed.
ISBN: 978-0-6151-3702-5 (pbk.)
1. Family & Relationships 2. Self-help 3. Religion

(What the book is really about: Faith, Hope, and Love)

SPECIAL SALES
This book is available at special discounts for bulk purchases for sales promotions or group events where a quantity of at least 10 copies are ordered. Special editions, including personalized covers and corporate imprints, can be easily created for special needs. For more information, write to Chris Miller, Help a Kid in Love, 4837 Farnam St., Omaha, NE 68132 or email chris@helpakidinlove.com.

 Hi, my name is Chris Miller and I love Steph. I am on a mission to tell the *entire* world that I love her, but I need your help. In this book you will discover the story that reveals why I love her so much and you can learn how you can tell the *entire* world that you love someone too.

I will also show you the most effective way to handle a broken heart, as I've been in the situation of having to let go of someone that I love more than life itself.

Will you please, "Help a Kid in Love?"

I'm a 21 year old college student from the small town of Mead, Nebraska, USA. One day I came up with a crazy idea to create a website that would allow me to show how much Steph means to me and help people of all ages get through the difficulties of losing a loved one. This book was spawned from the idea of that website and as I started writing it, the thought of actually telling the *entire* world that I love her miraculously came into being.

Before the creation of this book, I have never written or published an entire book, or had any experience whatsoever in doing something like this. My entire heart and soul went into the creation of the book and the website. I was pressed for time and money to write and print this book as soon as possible, so it may not be perfect. I feel, however, that I did my absolute best to make it my personal masterpiece when measured by effort and heart.

3

Help a Kid in Love

By Chris Miller

Donne ch'avete intelletto d'amore,

To every captive soul and gentle lover:

Please read my story,
and share with me your feelings
for I'd like to know:

Was there ever a man on this earth
who loved a woman so?

walk a mile with me,
and put yourself in my shoes;
before the last page

confidently you will ponder, "no"

"For where your treasure is,
there your heart will be also."

- Matthew 6:21

This book is for Steph; she is my treasure.

Table of Contents

Introduction – Tell the World You Love Someone

Chapter 1 – It's When You Care for Someone

Chapter 2 – From the Beginning

Chapter 3 – Out of the Clear Blue Sky

Chapter 4 – She's the One

Chapter 5 - My Treasure, My Proof

Chapter 6 – My Last Email

Chapter 7 - The Power and Endurance of Absolute Love

Chapter 8 - One Who Has Loved Truly, Can Never Lose Entirely

Chapter 9 – Help a Kid in Love

Acknowledgements

Help a Kid in Love

Tell the World You Love Someone

What would it take, to tell the entire world that you love someone? How much time would it take you to do it? How many people would you have to tell? How far would you have to travel? How loud would you have to yell? How many emails would you have to send? How many books would you have to write? How much money would you have to spend? Just how crazy would you have to be to actually try to tell the *entire* world that you are in love with the most beautiful person on the face of the earth?

If you have ever wondered how impossible it would be to tell the *entire* world something, or if you think I'm out of my mind to pose the question in the first place, I suggest you keep reading because I have found the solution. It is actually very simple. It might take a lot of work, but in a just one year, I will tell 25 people, speak in a normal tone of voice, send a few emails, write one book, not spend a dime, keep my sanity (what's left of it anyways), and within an incredibly short amount of time the *entire* world will know that I love Steph.

You probably think I'm out of my mind, but it is entirely possible for me to achieve my goal of telling the whole world that I love Steph. But I need your help. My website and the rest of the book explain how my plan of telling the *entire* world will work.

Will you help a kid in love?

If you do the math, 25 people, one book, and a few emails doesn't seem like it would come remotely close to reaching every individual on the planet. But I haven't finished explaining yet and haven't shown you the tricks up my sleeve. Before I give away my secret, I first want you to think about just how big the world is. The estimated world population is somewhere around 6.5 billion people. Six and a half billion is a huge number! It consists of a 6, a comma, a 5, followed by eight zeros, and two more commas. It looks like this:

$$6,500,000,000$$

I broke out my stop watch, timed myself, and it takes precisely 1.77 seconds to say the words, "I love Steph." Theoretically speaking, if you lined up every individual on the planet in a single file line, one by one at the rate of 1.77 seconds, it would take approximately 364 years, 208 days, 17 hours, 19 minutes, and 59 seconds to say, "I love Steph" 6.5 billion times in a row, back to back. No eating, no sleeping, no resting. No TV, no video games, no internet, no reading. One repetitive "I love Steph" after another. 1.77 seconds by 1.77 seconds, over and over again, 6.5 billion times. "I love Steph, I love Steph, I love Steph, I love Steph, I love Steph…" for 364 years! That's a long time! I've got some work to do.

Please continue reading as the rest of the book explains how I am cutting 364 years down to just a few. But more importantly, the rest of this book explains the passion behind it all that is making it happen.

Thank You

Thank you so much for taking the time to read what I have written. I hope you appreciate my thoughts, read with an open mind, and keep in mind that this is all coming from a 21 year-old kid who is trying to understand love and in the process has discovered the best way to get over the pain of a broken heart. To all of the younger readers, I hope you can learn from my experiences and hope that from my sharing them with you makes you a stronger, wiser, and kinder person.

To all the readers who have been on this earth longer than I have and those who may possess a deeper understanding of love, I would like to address that I am fully aware that there is much more for me to learn. You may be thinking to yourself, "What does a 21 year-old kid know about love?" All I can say, is to put yourself in my shoes and read this book in the light of a young man deeply in love. I will never claim that I know all there is to know about anything. However, through writing this book I have learned a lot about myself and learned a lot about the wonderful emotion of love. I am confident that you will enjoy reading my story. How often do you get to read an entire book that explains what is inside the heart and mind of a 21 year old guy?

The idea of this book and my website was originally intended as a Christmas gift for the love of my life. I simply wanted to do something that showed her just how much she means to me. As I started writing and sharing this book with others, I came to realize it had an intended reason for existing and needed to be shared with the *entire* world. Everyone needs to read this book. It doesn't matter how old you are, it doesn't matter where you live, it doesn't matter what situation you are in. You *are* going to be in love someday, or you are in love right now, or you have been in love before. No matter what, love is going to find you. And when it does, it is eventually going to put you through indescribable pain.

Relationships don't always work out like you want and people don't live forever. It's unavoidable. Someday, someone or something is going to break your heart. Maybe you are one of those lucky people who will find a significant other that never breaks up with you. Maybe you are part of the 50% of the population who will never have to go through a divorce. Maybe you have what it takes to make all your relationships go the distance. But even if you achieve everlasting love in all your relationships, someday you will have to attend a funeral of someone you love. Your friends, your parents, your brothers and sisters, your children, your grandparents, or your spouse…

> Stop for a second and put a picture in your mind of the few people in your life that you love more than anything.

It doesn't matter why you love them.
All that matters is that you care for them.

It's sad but true; they're not going to live forever. It would be wise to show them how much you love them while you're both alive, and it is beneficial to read this book so you can learn what to do when that day comes when you have to say goodbye to those you love.

Help a Kid in Love is more than a book and a story. It is a philosophy, a philosophy which allows any average person to turn the most hurtful experience of a broken heart into the most powerful and motivating source of energy known to the human race. It is a method which allows those who truly, purely, and absolutely love the one they lost to make the rest of their life just as fulfilling and just as exciting as it was before they had to suddenly let go of that special someone. This amazing source of energy and hope can be unlocked all without having to forget about the one you love and without having to go through the pain of "getting over" the love of your life. It allows you to retain the emotions of love without making them fade away, but at the same time allows you to move forward with your life and accept the unavoidable changes.

I advise you to read with caution as my philosophy crosses the lines of some sensitive subjects and goes against the grain of conventional relationship advice. It may influence you to make a committed choice you will have to live with for the rest your life, which in turn will give you a new way to see the important things which are often overlooked and ignored. If you have ever lost someone who you thought was "the one," or if you're just curious to know what it's like to go through the most painful experience of life, prepare yourself to find out how you can use your loss in a positive way that will allow you to make the rest of your dreams come true.

If you have never had the experience of a broken heart, this book may make you wish you had. Only those who have had to let go of something so special will be able to fully appreciate and understand the power of the words written. If anything can be learned from this book, I hope it is that you learn to use your love instead of fighting to hide it.

There are two extreme choices you can make after your heart breaks. You can let it ruin you, or you can harness the pain and use it as a tool to change the world and enrich your life. I hope you learn to use the pain rather than trying to cover it up. This book will show you how to make the best of lost love, and is beneficial to anyone who reads it. Hopefully it will provide the courage, hope, support, uplift, and positive mental attitude to those in the world who need it most.

I would like to extend to you a world of gratitude and thanks from the bottom of my heart just for holding this book in your hand. If you would like to ask me any questions or if you would like to share your thoughts, comments, or concerns feel free to do so by logging on to my website at www.HelpaKidinLove.com. I would also like to personally thank each and every individual who has contributed to my goal of telling the entire world that I love Steph. If you have yet to do so, please sign up on my website at so I can personally send out my thanks to you.

I wish you all the success and happiness in your own life. If you ever need help with anything at all, if there is ever anything troubling you, never be afraid to think outside the box and ask the entire world to help you out.

Sincerely, with all the love in the world,

                Christopher Glen Miller
                www.HelpaKidinLove.com
                Mead, Nebraska, USA
                December 25, 2006

Help a Kid in Love

Chapter 1

It's When You Care for Someone

Writing and finishing this book has been the most physically demanding, time consuming, energy draining, and thought provoking venture of my life. Never before have I worked on a project that has brought out so many emotions and taught me so much. It was a lot of work getting this finished, but there was no way I was going to give up on a book that the *entire* world needs to read. It was also impossible for me to give up. It was gut-wrenching and exciting to think I was about to launch a mission which has never been attempted in human history. Never before has anyone purposely tried to tell the entire world that they love someone. It's such a simple idea too. I really can't believe no one has ever tried it. "I'm telling the *entire* world who I love." It has such a nice ring to it.

Maybe one out of the billions of people alive today, or one of the trillions who have lived on this earth in the past has actually tried to tell the *entire* world who they love. If such an attempt had been made, it was not completely fulfilled as they failed to tell me. I'm usually the last one to find out any sort of news, so it just might be the case that everyone except me knows about someone else that tried to tell the entire world who they love. Not once have I ever personally seen of or heard of, such an attempt. So if someone had in fact set out on a mission to tell the whole world, they weren't 100% successful because the message didn't reach me.

What also grabs my attention about this goal is that if someone actually committed to set out on a mission to tell the *entire* world that they love someone, how could they not find a way to do it? If there was any idea, any task, any goal, any challenge to be pursued, I can think of no better thing to make it all happen than love. If that person was truly and absolutely in love to the deepest degree, how could they not find a way? Love always finds a way.

Throughout this book you will learn just how passionate I am about the woman I love, and you will discover why I think I'm the perfect candidate to be the first person in history to tell the *entire* world who they love. While I'm at it, I would also like to give you the opportunity to tell the entire world who *you* love. Through my website, you can join in on my mission. This is history in the making and I want you to be a part of it. Plus I'm going to need your help in order for me to reach my goal. In return for your help, I can't think of anything more valuable to give to you than the chance to be part of history.

As a side note to making a mark in the books of time, I would also like to find out how so many amazing couples in this world make their relationships last. It has been written that passion is anger and love combined. By that definition, my mission truly is a quest of passion. Half of me is angry at the fact that on more than one occasion, I've been part of the most perfect relationships that just seem to go down the drain even after I did everything I could to give my best and make sure they lasted. There are so many happy couples in this world who have been together for years. I want to know what makes it all stick together, as it gets frustrating not having the missing piece of the puzzle.

Besides the anger, the other half of me consists of nothing but absolute love. It's going to take boatloads of elbow grease, and it will be the journey of a lifetime for me to tell the whole world what's in my heart. Luckily I've experienced absolute love. There isn't anything that can get in my way. You're about to discover the unstoppable power of love. If you read with an open mind and heart, you will quickly begin to share my confidence and optimism.

After I had the first rough draft of the book completed, I was wrestling with a dissatisfaction that nearly ruined everything. Here I was with my book on love that I was about to share with the *entire* world. But there was one very large problem. If someone is going to tell the entire world that they love someone, they better have full understanding of what the word love means. I poured my entire heart into the rough draft, researched every book and article on love that I had time for, and asked countless numbers of people. But I still couldn't completely, simply, and fundamentally explain what love is. I wanted it, experienced it, lost it, researched it, wrote a book about it, and could feel it on the inside, so I had a general idea. However, I couldn't sum it up in just a few words. Getting to the core of the way I understand love was something I *had* to do before I was going to let anyone else read my book. It was at the tip of my tongue, but I just couldn't find the right words to explain it.

One day I was sitting at my computer scratching my head, digging for an answer of how I could completely yet simply explain love in its totality. My writing and my thoughts were going nowhere, but I wasn't going to give up. I had everything in place to make history. I had a book, a website, a written and drawn out plan, and a whole lot of faith. I was just one simple explanation away from launching into the stratosphere of history making. But I wasn't about to tell the entire world who I love, when I couldn't fully explain what love really is. Without such a simple explanation, history could've still been made, but it would've been just one colossal lie. "I love Steph. I don't know what love is, but I love her, and I'm trying to tell the *entire* world." That just wouldn't make sense and I couldn't live with myself knowing I made history via one big lie.

As I was biting my fingernails, nervous about missing out on my chance to do something spectacular, my four year-old, energy factory of a sister comes waltzing into my room. Interrupting me and my writing is one of her favorite pastimes. I usually just shrugged her off and made her leave my room when I was hard at work. But for some odd reason, I actually took the time to give her some attention.

I inquired, "So what are you up to Abby? Are you staying out of trouble?"

"Yes," she said with her innocent grin, "I was just upstairs watching TV." I asked her what she was watching and she said, "It's this show on ABC about this like family." (Her older sister gave her the bad habit of overusing the word *like*.)

It was always my concern that the television would just rot her brain out so I always quiz her to see if it's productive. "So what do you learn from watching that show?" I asked her.

She said, "Well, you learn, like, you learn like how to take care of a family."

"So, how do you take care of a family?" I was just asking for fun now.

"You feed em, and give em hugs."

"Give em hugs?"

"No, you give em love," she explained as I misheard.

To continue my fun little quiz, I asked Abby who she loves. She just grinned and said, "I love you, and I love my mom, and I love my dad."

In the middle of our conversation I remembered that I desperately needed to find a simple explanation of what love is. There was no time to be wasting talking to a four year-old. There was work to do and history to be made. Sorry Abby, I really need to solve this problem first. I turned to my computer and took another look at everything I had written. After taking a deep breath I whispered to myself, "Love, what's that?" I was just whispering out loud to myself trying to get my brain back into thinking mode. Abby was still standing there and overhead what I whispered. She must have thought I was still quizzing her and she replied, "It's when you care for someone." As soon as she said it she just started skipping out of my room.

Hmmm... It's when you care for someone. I thought about it for awhile and realized she was absolutely right. When you think about love, in any situation, it truly does boil down to caring about them. If you have a significant other, you love them simply because you care about them. If you love anything at all, whether it's a person, place, or thing, it all starts from the fact that you care about whatever it is you love.

Help a Kid in Love

You may not even have a specific reason as to *why* you care about them, you just do. And above all, you care about them all while not expecting anything in return. Abby didn't say, "It's when you care for someone and they care for you too." All she said was, "It's when *you* care for someone." After she said it, I couldn't find any logical reason that proved her wrong. As soon as I realized she was right, a mix of excitement and relief set in as I now had a simple, effective, and completely true way of explaining what love is.

"That's it!" I yelled, "It's when you care for someone!" Why hadn't I thought of that? What is love? It's when you care for someone. Simple, effective, complete, absolutely true; and it all came from the mind of a four year-old. I had spent months trying to figure this out and it took Abby less than a split second to spit out the words, "It's when you care for someone." She left the room before I could say anything else to her, almost as giving me the answer of a lifetime was the only reason she waltzed into my room in the first place. I was so excited and wanted to give her a huge hug to thank her for giving me a perfect answer to a question that not only me, but much of mankind has been beating themselves up over since the beginning of time. What is love? It's when you care for someone. Genius! Before I could respond, she had vanished. Thanks Abby, wherever you went!

Now I'm set. Now I can make history. Now I can do something that has never, ever been done. Now, thanks to my four year-old sister, I can simply and effectively explain what love is in just a few words. Now I can tell the *entire* world that I love one very special person because I CARE FOR HER!

Chris Miller

Chris Loves Steph!

Pass it on!

HelpaKidinLove.com

I've Decided to Stick with Love

Before I get into telling you the story about what set me on my mission of telling the *entire* world that I love someone, I first need to mention my purpose and answer a few questions to ease some concerns, set the record straight, and assure you that I am not insane, just in love. There are so many reasons for writing this book and creating my website, but the underlying purpose of their creation was simply my way of showing Steph what she means to me. Hopefully my actions will inspire you to take chances, forget about failure, and follow your heart.

There are lots of ways to show people what they mean to you. But when that person really does mean the world to you, showing them so requires more than a Hallmark card and more than a bouquet of flowers. Telling all 6.5 billion people that I love Steph is my way of showing her that there isn't anything else on the planet that means more to me than she does.

Telling all 6.5 billion people is also my BHAG (Bee-Hag), which stands for Big, Hairy, Audacious, Goal. This acronym was created by Jim Collins in his book, *Built to Last*. The term was created to provide individuals, companies, and organizations a unifying focal point of effort, and it acts as a catalyst to achieve greatness. I encourage everyone in the world today to set their own BHAG and take actions to move closer to the goal no matter how large it is. I can say from experience, life will be much fuller, more meaningful, and way more exciting once someone sets and pursues a gi-normous (gigantic and enormous) goal that is based upon something you are passionate about.

BHAG is my new favorite thing to say. Ever since I was little, I wanted to do something that has never been done before. The desire was always there to be different-to achieve something great. By writing down my BHAG, my dream of doing something that no one else has ever done is now that much closer to reality. Taking the steps to achieve it has given me the feeling that I can accomplish anything when I set my mind *and* my heart to it. Thanks to one big broken heart and one big, hairy, audacious goal, I realized that I can make a difference in this world even though I'm just a kid.

It was brought to my attention that writing a book like this and pursuing my big, hairy, audacious goal may send the wrong message that would put much unneeded stress and attention on Steph which she might not appreciate. I also received concerns from people that I may appear to be some type of stalker! I was thoroughly alarmed when the word stalker was used in the same sentence as my name. Steph and I have been friends ever since I can remember, and we are still friends to this day. She knows me well enough to know that I'm not that type of creepy person.

I realize that you cannot force someone to love you. There is no intention to influence her to take action, nor am I intending to put any type of unwanted attention or pressure on her. All I want to do is ensure she knows what she means to me and tell the world what it's like to be in love to the deepest degree. To set the record straight, this is not some desperate attempt to win her back. By the end of the book you will discover that I *have* moved on and am not "dwelling" on the past. Parts of what you read throughout the first five chapters was written before I discovered the best way to handle a broken heart. When you read, it may appear that I am still attached. Keep in mind that this book was written while I was actually going through the rough times and experiencing the process of a broken heart. Although there are many books about this same subject, all of them I've read did not seem to be written during the heat of the moment. And I highly doubt you have the opportunity anywhere else to read what is inside the heart of a 21 year-old guy.

This book and my quest is a devoted expression of gratitude for everything Steph has given to me, most importantly some very important life lessons including having the courage to take chances and make changes. I have already discussed everything with her. At first she said, "You're going to do what?" But once I explained it all to her she just smiled, and said, "If you think this is what you were meant to do, then it is ok with me."

I also received concerns and comments (if you know the basic storyline you might agree) that I have some serious issues to deal with, and it may even appear I am dealing with them in an entirely wrong way. Yes it is true, Steph doesn't love me back like she used to, and yes I would still like to tell the *entire* world that I love her. Right now it might not make sense to you why on earth I would want to do that, but unconventional thinking is the overarching message I'm trying to send with this book. By the end, you will understand (and hopefully appreciate) my reasons for doing what I'm doing. I discovered that in order to move on from losing the one person you love more than life itself, you must continue loving them without hiding your feelings. You may not understand it completely at the moment, but I hope you try to put yourself in the shoes of someone who has been in love with one person for nearly three-fourths of their entire lifetime, and then one day wakes up to see that special someone disappear.

In response to your concern that I have a serious issue, I would slightly disagree. It is true, I *had* a very serious issue, and I *was* having an incredibly difficult time dealing with it. This book shows how I dealt with the most painful experience of my life in a way no one else has ever recommended. It can act as a guide for you to do the same if your heart has been broken to the deepest degree.

As you will discover, besides being the biggest fan of Steph, I am also a huge fan of Jim Collins and Napoleon Hill. These authors, in conjunction with Steph, my parents, my friends, my teachers, and other role models have provided me with the most valuable asset on the planet which is a positive mental attitude which allows me to strive to achieve my BHAG. In Mr. Collins' second book, *Good to Great*, he mentions the importance to face the brutal facts before launching into pursuit of your BHAG.

You may be thinking to yourself that my goal of telling the *entire* world is impossible. If you're an optimistic person, at best you are probably thinking that it will take a miracle to tell *EVERYONE*. You may also say that I should just move on and live my life like a normal person would do. "There are plenty of fish in the sea, why limit yourself to just one?" I've heard it all including that I must be nuts to try to tell the *entire* world something in one lifetime.

My response to all of the above… You're absolutely right! It *is* going to take a miracle to tell every person on the face of the earth one single message. Not only do I have to translate my message into hundreds of different languages, I also have to keep up with the 2.5 people who are born every second of every day around the entire globe. You are also absolutely right that there are plenty of other fish in the sea that might make me just as happy as Steph does. But you know what, she's *the* fish. She's that one special fish that I've spent more than two-thirds of my entire life trying to catch. Eventually I finally did catch her, but had to release her back into the big blue ocean much too soon.

So far in my life, she's that one special person that no matter what happens, a part of me will always be in love with her. The type of love may be different from when we were together, but nevertheless I will always care for her. Throughout the book, you will learn how to get through hard times all while never having to stop loving that special someone who suddenly had to say goodbye. As a matter of fact, I am now "going fishing." I do keep my options open, but at the same time I know a part of me will always love Steph. To solve this problem, I have simply stopped trying to fight it.

"I've decided to stick with love."
- Dr. Martin Luther King Jr.

My goal of telling the *entire* world that I love Steph might stand a sliver of chance of becoming a reality. However, I have unwavering faith that love and ambition are the two most important ingredients to make anything happen in this world, including miracles! If there is one message possible of spanning the entire earth, what better message to spread than that of love? What better person to start that message than a 21 year old kid, who you will find out later, is the epitome of average?

Love is the catalyst for miracles. Countless achievements performed in the history of mankind have been propelled by some form of love. Throughout the book you will find many great achievements sparked from love. Abraham Lincoln ended slavery after he went through his heartbreaking struggles with his young love for his dear Ann Rutledge. Dante's "The Divine Comedy" was written in the 1300's from the point of view of Dante himself, who divinely cherished his beloved Beatrice ever since he was nine years old. His literary works are considered some of the best of all time and are credited for being the first great works produced during the Renaissance. Dante and Lincoln are just two small examples of what the wonderful, powerful, and unstoppable emotions of love can accomplish.

Chris Miller

Next to every great man in the universe,
stands a great woman, whom he loves dearly.

Underlying Principle

People who are under the mad influence of love often do insane things when the one they love stops loving them back. Much of the loved-and-lost population go into a deep depression, cry for a long time, lose a lot of sleep, mope, gripe, take their loss out on other people, and think of reasons they were done wrong. In very rare and extreme cases some people go as far to threaten suicide, and unfortunately some have actually executed their threat.

I can relate to all of those people I have just mentioned. However, one thing is entirely different between those mentioned and myself. I have been deeply, deeply in love, and it might seem like I have lost in every way possible. Luckily I have experienced absolute love and haven't lost an ounce of what I had to start with. I don't get to be with the person I love everyday, and although she doesn't love me back like she used to, there isn't a single thing in the *entire* world that has the power to stop me from loving her, except for myself.

It is incredibly easy for me to relate to anyone who has lost that one special something that they love more than anything else. However, I cannot relate to how so many people allow the greatest feeling in the world to disappear, or worse yet, channel the most powerful force in the universe into something negative. After hitting rock bottom, as others might describe it, I have made the choice to make the absolute best of the situation.

Towards the end of the book, you will find out that it is solely your choice on how to handle your broken heart. It was my choice to write a book and create a website founded on the principles of love. Both the book and the website have the potential to change the world and make it a better place by simply spreading the message of love. This book was written for three ultimate reasons. First, I want Steph to know what she means to me. Second, I want the *entire* world to know what absolute love is like. And third, I would like to show the *entire* world the best way to handle a broken heart. The first three chapters lead up to my relationship with Steph, the next three reveal how wonderful it was to be with her, and the last three disclose the most efficient way I have found to handle a heart that has been broken to the deepest degree.

The best attempt will be made to show you what true, enduring, absolute love is like. Absolute love will be explained in greater detail in the rest of the book. Throughout the chapters you will find out how great love is, how good it can feel, how bad it can hurt, how it can make you smile, make you laugh, make you cry, and make you do crazy things you never thought you would ever do. When it gets a hold of you, absolute love is something that makes you believe in things you can't see, allows you to do what you never thought possible, and opens your eyes to so many wonderful things in life that are completely hidden to the eyes of someone who has yet to experience it.

Love is the underlying principle of anything good in this world. It is the by-product of most spectacular beauty. It promotes trust, friendship, companionship, compassion, concern, tenderness, sympathy, faith, affection, devotion, and loyalty. It provides the greatest feeling of warmth, gives you emotions you will forever hold dear, and provides memories that will never pass. It is the ultimate synergy of all the most genuinely good things in life.

Chances are, and I really do hope, that you have experienced love before. It may be a person, your spouse, your family, a pastime, a place, or some other thing. Feelings of love have the ability to affect you in all of the senses, and even beyond the five physical senses. Although it is something that begins and ends as an emotion, along the way it encompasses all of the five senses. All of the soothing aromas you can smell, the sweetest tastes you can savor, the most gorgeous sights you can see, the most exquisite sounds you can hear, and the most pleasant objects you can touch. Besides impacting the physical senses, it also has the power to take complete control over one's thoughts and actions without the human body having the slightest clue of what is going on. At the time of my writing this, I am 21 years old. I never could have written an entire book, let alone get it published, and distributed without the inspiring influence of love.

The ironic thing about it all, is that love can spark certain feelings and heightens all of your bodily senses without having anything physically present. It has the amazing ability to operate on its own, entirely independent of everything else in the universe. It requires no source of energy and needs no frame of reference. It cannot be measured, it cannot be compared, and even though I am making a concerted effort to do so, it can not be fully reduced to mere words.

The rest of the book is simply a description of what I've personally been through, what I've personally felt, and how I harnessed the power of absolute love. All the words you read are an honest and vivid description of everything that lives inside my heart. All of the following stories are true to my best knowledge and have not been distorted in any form whatsoever. Every word you read in this book derived from utter, complete, unconditional, and absolute love.

From here, I will ask you of two huge favors. First, please continue reading. You will be interested in what is written. And second, I am about to ask you the biggest favor I have asked of anyone in my entire life. The last chapter provides a guide that specifically shows how you can help me reach my goal of telling the *entire* world that I love Steph and also reveals how you can share your amazing stories of love and make history with me. The world needs your help. In this last chapter, there are specific descriptions of what you can do to help not only me, but many others in the world who are in absolute love and need your help. I encourage you to read the book straight through without skipping to the end. If you read everything from the beginning, you may not even have to read the last chapter, as you will already know what you can do to help a kid in love.

Help Me, I'm in Love!

It's 3:00 AM on a Sunday morning and I'm speeding as fast as I can to get to a Wal-Mart. I NEED to get these sunglasses. I just need them. Without them, everything is lost. My entire life, my entire future depends upon the biggest and shiniest pair of silver-rimmed sunglasses I can find. You know what they look like. They are the ones that U.S. Air Force pilots wear. I am in dire need of a pair of shades that look just like the ones that Tom Cruise sported in the movie Top Gun.

> *"Emily! I need your help! Will you do me a favor?*
> *This might sound like a weird question to ask,*
> *but can you call me when Steph comes home?*
> *You have to promise to keep it a secret that I called."*

Emily is Steph's little sister, and is one of the very first individuals to help a kid in love. She was on my team, and was a huge help in the effort to win Steph back. Maybe "win back" is the wrong phrase to use. First of all, love is not a contest that can be won or lost. And secondly, I did nothing wrong to lose her in the first place. I always did everything to ensure she knew how much I loved her. From day one it was my top priority to treat her like a queen and a princess. As cliché as that sounds, that is exactly what she is to me and is exactly how she deserves to be treated. At any rate I couldn't believe to be in the position of having to let go of something so precious. I was the luckiest person on the face of the earth to be with her in the first place, but I was willing to do anything within my human power to stop the separation from happening.

Here's my game plan. I'm going to buy these goofy sunglasses, memorize the words to "You've Lost that Loving Feeling" by the Righteous Brothers, wait for her to come home, drive out to her house, put on my goofy glasses that look nowhere near the real thing, throw on a CD, make a complete fool out of myself, get on one knee, and sing to her, karaoke-style, using a television remote control for a microphone. By the end of the song she'll realize she's "lost that loving feeling" and she needs to change her mind. PERFECT! It's a brilliant idea! Maybe it's not 100% original, maybe someone else in the world has actually tried this same desperate attempt, but anyways, I am so incredibly positive this plan is going to work…

I wish it were that easy. As it turns out, driving like it's the dawn of Armageddon to get to a Wal-Mart that's open 24 hours a day and staying up all night to make sure I know the lines to a song I already had memorized in the first place, somehow, someway, it turns out that it just wasn't enough. I know my voice isn't the greatest and last time I checked in the mirror, I would not pass as a double for Tom Cruise, but the performance was perfect. After what I thought was a splendid serenade attempt, there was no response in return.

The one thing that provided satisfaction, even though I didn't change her mind, was the fact that I made her smile. (Making her smile is by far my favorite thing to do.) I think Emily thought it was funny too. I had just made an absolute fool out of myself in front of the two sweetest girls I know, and I couldn't care less if it sounded and looked funny, awkward, or weird. It was obvious they could sense my sincerity. Or maybe they were just in awe that I was making such a fool of myself.

But something about the look on Steph's face was telling me, "I can't believe you're actually doing this, because it's not going to help." I could tell, or at least I thought I could, that nothing I attempted would have changed her mind. That didn't matter. I didn't want to hear it, and I didn't believe it. I was, and still am to this day, incapable of not loving this girl.

Chapter 2

From the Beginning…

(Within the first five chapters, you will find some of my **Hea**lthy **R**elationship **T**ips sprinkled throughout the text that you can use to make the most of your relationships, whether they last forever or not.)

> (**Hea**lthy **R**elationship **T**ip) **HeaRT #1**: First, realize who loves you before you love others

Writing a book about love without mentioning my family would be a tragedy. First of all, I wouldn't exist if it my parents didn't love each other. But more importantly, I wouldn't know how to love another person if it weren't for my mom and dad. They are my greatest role models here on earth. They have given me so much support and love throughout my entire life, and through it all they have never asked, demanded or expected me to give them anything back in return. That is what absolute love is all about.

My parents are amazing people. I don't know how they pulled it off, but they raised a responsible, loving family all while being the least strict of parents who always allowed their kids a great deal of freedom and always let us do what we thought was important. They only stepped in at the critical moments when my siblings and I started to veer in the wrong direction. I was always amazed and always felt sorry for my friends who had parents that watched over every little thing they did and demanded their children do certain things with their life that the *parents* thought was most important.

Rather than telling me what to do with my life, my parents just sat back, watched me grow, and never stopped loving me for a second. They are the principal reason which allowed me to write a book about love. I am only 21 years old, never published a book in my life, and have never read any books about love until recently. I cannot claim to be an expert on the subject of love, but I have been exposed to two people who have mastered it and shown me by example my entire life and have given me nothing but absolute love from the day I was born. They provided all the support and affection needed for me to understand love to the point where I could write a book about it.

I am the middle child of a family of five. My older brother Adam is 24, older sister Angie is 23, I am 21, my younger sister Carol is 15, and my youngest sister Abby is 4. No, that is not a typo; I have a 24 year old brother and a four year old sister. After 20 years of having their first child, my parents thought they were doing such a good job with their first four kids that they saw no harm in having a fifth! I'll never forget the day they told us about Abby. My mom and dad were 40 years old at the time, and Adam, Angie, Carol, and I thought they were nuts and were enraged they would do such a thing. We liked our family just the way it was. We didn't need a little brat running around the house in diapers! How wrong we were. Abby has been another blessing to our family.

My parents have been true to each other since day one. They were married young, started their family young, and continue loving each other and their kids as each day passes. Without a doubt they will be incredible grandparents. Angie just broke the news to us that she is having her first child of her own which will make my parents grandparents for the first time in their life.

My mom and dad went to the same high school and live in the same small town where I have been born and raised my entire life. They dated throughout high school and are the perfect high school sweetheart couple. I always thought, and wanted too, that I would end up just like them. Seeing how they had ended up made me expect that things would happen the same way to me. Someday I would meet someone in school, fall in love with them, get married, and start raising a happy family of my own. They made it look so easy, and I could see how happy they were, so it made me want to be just like them.

> **HeaRT #2**: Try not to *assume* certain things will happen

I Was Born in Small Town

The first 21 years of my life took place in the small town of Mead, Nebraska, USA. The town of Mead sits in the middle of everywhere, but seems like the middle of nowhere. It is 1,500 miles east of Los Angeles, 1,300 miles west of New York, 1,200 miles north of southern-most tip of Texas, and 600 miles south of the Canadian border. My hometown is just about in the center of the United States. Even within the state of Nebraska, Mead is right in the middle of the major population concentrations. My hometown is right in the middle of the largest, second largest, and sixth largest cities in the state.

Although it is in the middle of everywhere, it often feels like the middle of nowhere. The nice thing about a the village of Mead is that it is a quiet town that doesn't have to put up with the hustle and bustle of the city, but is always just a short drive away if there is ever anything needed from the grocery store or shopping mall.

Even from a kid's standpoint the house I grew up in was, for the most part, you guessed it, right in the middle of town. My dad built our house in walking distance between the elementary school, the high school, the baseball field, and the park. For all I was concerned, I was in the center of the universe. Also, as I mentioned earlier I am the middle child of the family. Middle of the U.S., middle of Nebraska, middle of town, middle of the family, you might as well just refer to me from now on as Mr. Middle!

Growing up, there were three distinct traits that I began to develop. Curiosity, building, and pain were three things that I seemed naturally attracted to. One of my favorite books I enjoyed reading when I was little was *The Way Things Work*. It was this big book that had pictures and descriptions about how just about everything in the world works. That book taught me everything from the science of inertia to the inner workings of a toilet. The only thing missing from that book was "the way relationships work." Unfortunately there is no crash course for kids on the subject of relationships. This is another important reason for the creation of *Help a Kid in Love*.

The Way Things Work developed my early interest in science and math. What drew me into these two subjects was proof. No matter what the theory was, no matter what teachers in school were trying to teach me, it could be backed with proof. Science, math, and understanding the way things work coincides with my hobby of building things. My desire to build started with my Lego collection. Days on end were spent meticulously putting projects together until they were just right. Sometimes I would follow the directions, but most of the time I would just do things the way I saw fit, and learned as I built.

My brother and I usually put together our buildings together. Having an older brother who always included me is one of the reasons I developed a common acquaintance with pain. His friends were not only older, but also much bigger than me. I got hurt so much playing with him and his friends that I almost got to the point where I didn't care how much pain was involved as long I had fun doing whatever it was that I loved to do. To this day, I am still trying to find out how everything in the world works, am always working on my next project, and more often than not, find myself running head on into pain.

One of the Many Chris Miller's

I'm an average kid from an average town who has a very common name. I would be curious to find out how many "Chris Miller's" are in the world today. My parents might as well have named me John Smith! When I grew up I collected lots of football and baseball cards. It was so cool to collect all of the Chris Miller cards. There was a quarterback who played for the Atlanta Falcons that shared my name. I would always joke around, and say, "Hey look! I'm on a football card! That's really me!"

Today, it is not so exciting to see other people with the same name as me. There are times it is actually ridiculous how common of a name I have. One day I had an interview scheduled for an internship and the interviewer had to ask me what my middle name was. I was thinking to myself, "Why do you care what my middle name is?" Then she said, "We have another Chris Miller we are interviewing today so I just need to make sure I don't mix you up." What are the odds!? The same day, the same company, the same position, the same name! How belittling!

One night I went out with my friends to celebrate our classmate's 21st birthday and I introduced myself to some of her friends. After I told them my name, they mentioned that they have two other friends by the name of Chris Miller. And just a few days after that, I got a phone call from one of my other buddies from high school. He left a voice mail that said something along the lines of, "Chris, this is Brendan, I'm waiting for you, where in the heck are you at?" I hadn't talked to Brendan for a few weeks so immediately I called him back and asked him what his message was all about. His reply, "whoops, I meant to call the *other* Chris Miller I know." I asked him if he was serious, and it turns out it was an honest mistake of calling the wrong person with the same name.

So here I am. One of the many Chris Miller's of the world from a small town smack dab in the middle of the USA, in the middle of the larger surrounding towns, who grew up in a house in the middle of the town, and am the middle child of the family to boot. I'm just an extremely average kid trying to tell the *entire* world who I love. I hope you can help me out.

Shared Background

> **HeaRT #3**: Having a common background is not necessary, but it is very beneficial

Steph and I grew up in a small town consisting of roughly 500 residents, a small bank, a town pub, a diner, a gas station (founded by my grandpa), a convenience store, a fire department, a village office, two baseball fields (one built by my father), a post office, an elementary school, and a high school. The town is small, quiet, and peaceful. Steph and I spent our entire childhood growing up there, and it is the one place we both call home.

We were in the same class ever since kindergarten. The first time I felt attraction for Steph was in the first grade. I was too young to know what to do about it or how to understand what I was feeling, but there was definitely something inside me saying that this girl was something special. She was the type of girl who naturally lit up the room. She had a pretty face, wore a huge smile, had the cutest laugh, a sparkle in her eye, and long, curly bleach blond hair. And I had a crush. Had I not been so distracted with all the toys, boxes of crayons, and lessons on tying my shoes, I probably would have asked her to marry me, but I was too busy to think about that.

From the first grade on, there were many similarities Steph shared with me. We both had a tendency to hang around the kids in the grade above us, and we both usually took on the role of being leaders in our own class. We both were talented athletes. Steph was a little better than me at sports, but I made up for it on the academic end. To this day she still calls me a geek. I never told her, but I actually kind of like it when she calls me a geek, don't ask me why, I don't even know.

My dad and Steph's mom had also graduated in the same class from Mead High School and both of our families are close friends in and out of school activities. Our families frequently visit each other and attend many of the same events. Over the years we have spent a fair amount of time at each other's houses.

Hanging out at Steph's House

> **HeaRT #4**: Love is always stronger with a solid foundation of friendship

I always had a blast at Steph's house. She lived in the country so there was always something fun to do. In her backyard there was a pool and a trampoline, and across the road were a small pond and a stream. Her house was paradise for a curious and adventurous kid like me. I had so much fun riding their four-wheeler around their farm and swimming in their pond and wading in their pool and just hanging out.

One time we were out swimming in the pond and we got into a huge mud fight. It was me and Steph's brother vs. my sister and Steph. Boys vs. girls, all out war! The battle went on for about half an hour. The trick was to be able to stay underneath the water and then come up for air in a quick enough fashion to throw your mud ball and then quickly duck back under the water to avoid the onslaught of flying masses of mud headed directly towards your face. My timing was off when I came up for air one time, and a huge hunk of mud, directly from Steph's hand, pounded me squarely on the side of my face. The mud ball was caked to the side of my face and had splattered just enough to blanket most of my eye and my entire ear on the left side of my head.

I retaliated just as any 11 year-old boy would do. Revenge! Throw it back! The mud fight came to a sudden halt when my sister came up from under the surface and yelled out, "Look what I found!" When she went down to reach for a handful of mud, she had dug up a clamshell! How a clamshell ends up in a Nebraska pond I do not know. But our mud battle soon turned into a science experiment.

We rushed back to Steph's house, rinsed off all the mud and immediately put the clam in a bucket. "What should we do we do with it?" we were asking ourselves. "Should we keep it as a pet? What should we name it? Maybe we should open it? What if there's a pearl inside!" Our excitement and curiosity was struck with the hope of getting something of value from our treasure found in the mud. We tried breaking it open by hand, but had no luck. So with butter knife in hand, I began prying open our treasure and to our avail... nothing was inside. There was no pearl, and none of us had the appetite for Midwestern clams, so we called it quits and went inside.

A week later I was still digging out dried up chunks of mud in my ear from the mud ball that Steph had pelted me with. A glob of flying mud is about as far from Cupid's arrows as you can get, but somehow it had the same affect. Whenever I went out to her house, I was there to play with her younger brother, but in the back of my mind I always wished I could be spending more time with her. Although, I always had a crush on her, and spent a lot of time at her house and with her family, I never told her how I felt about her while we were growing up.

I would go back and forth from being in love with her to convincing myself she wouldn't be interested in me. Throughout grade school and junior high, I would either be head over heels in love with her (and of course too afraid to do anything about it) or I would convince myself that there is no way she wanted to have anything to do with me. By the time I was a freshman in high school, I had convinced myself that there was no way Steph would ever like me and concluded that girls were a waste of time, and I should focus on more important things like basketball.

Chris Miller

> **HeaRT #5**: Never be afraid to speak up.
> If you never ask, the answer is always "no"

Sophomores and Juniors

I vividly remember a few occasions during our sophomore and junior years in high school where I came so close to asking her out. At the end of our sophomore year, I was on the track team and she was playing softball. My biggest achievement that year was making it to the state meet in the two mile run. I was wiry and skinny so it meant a lot to me to be able to achieve any type of athletic feat. Running at the state track meet was one of the most nerve racking experiences of my life.

On the track, you are surrounded by thousands of spectators in the grandstands from all over the state, and when you look around you see waves of the toughest competition you face the entire season. As it was my first time, I was scared to death when I was lining up at the starting line waiting for the gun to go off. But eventually the race started and the apprehension went away and I had the time of my life ending up finishing in 10th place.

I didn't win the race, but I was proud to go through the experience and was proud of putting forth my absolute best effort, even though I didn't win. Since I didn't win a medal, the souvenir of pride I went away with was a 4 inch by 5 inch sticker with the number 32, which represented my lane assignment which was worn on my shorts. This sticker was the only thing I could keep as a memory from my proud achievement so I made sure I was going to hold on to it, and keep it around forever.

When I got home that same day from the track meet Steph was at my house standing in the driveway. She was there to hang out with my sister. She was holding some of her softball gear in her hand, and I noticed her jersey number was #14, which was the same as my basketball jersey number. I said something stupid along the lines of, "sweet number, you rock!" Then ironically she saw my sticker from the track meet, and she said, "Sweet number, you rock!" and smiled. Number 32 was her basketball jersey number. What are the odds! How weird, we said, that we are both holding each other's basketball numbers in our hands.

We stopped and talked about how the track meet went and I asked how her softball season was going. We started talking about other things too and eventually started laughing. Before I knew it, I took my souvenir of pride and stuck it on her shorts, and said, "Here, this is your number, it belongs to you." I couldn't believe I just did that! That was my keepsake of my first state track meet, and she's probably just going to throw it away when she gets home, it's just a sticker to her. But it really didn't matter. I would have let her throw anything of mine away to have that one conversation with her, even though it only lasted a few minutes.

> **HeaRT #6**: If it is love you seek, be prepared to give everything you have to get nothing in return

Later that summer, Steph ran into me again when I was working my summer job. My dad owns a lawn mowing business. It was my job to mow the school grounds in the summer. On the mower I always wore a big pair of noise blocking headphones, so I was usually unaware of anything but the grass in front of me that needed to be mowed.

One day I was mowing the practice football field which had a row of pine trees separating it from the parking lot. From the corner of my eye, I saw somebody walking through the line of trees. "What's somebody doing out here?" I was wondering to myself. And eventually I noticed it was Steph! Now I really started to wonder. What is *she* doing out here. I was about 40 yards away from the trees so I just kept mowing, pretending that I didn't even see her. But then I noticed she was walking towards me! My heart stopped. She smiled and waved at me. Then my heart started going backwards! Why on earth is she walking my way? My mind almost went so numb that I nearly forgot that she waved to me. So I quickly made the most awkward wave of my life hoping she didn't realize how nervous I was.

Eventually she came right up to me. I had stopped the mower so it was quiet enough to talk to her, and we just started talking. She said she saw me and just thought she would come over and say hi. We weren't even talking about anything that important, but I have never been more nervous in a conversation. We talked about how each other's summer had been going, and I promised her that I would make it to one of her softball games someday. All in all it was a brief conversation, but I will never forget how she just smiled through all of it. There's something about the way she smiles that just makes you melt on the spot. I will always remember the feeling in my stomach when I saw an angel emerging from the trees and then walking my way. She never even had to say anything; she just had to show up to make my heart start beating faster.

> **HeaRT #7**: Communication is vital; however, sometimes a presence is enough to make a heart beat faster

Unbelievably Talented

Luckily, my sister played on the same softball team as Steph, so it always gave me a reason to be able to go watch her without anyone knowing the real reason I was at those softball games. Steph is an amazing pitcher. She can throw a barrage of different breaking balls, and has a mean fastball. I would be very scared to stand at the plate against her. Watching her pitch is a thing of beauty. There's something about the way she does it, her graceful movements, which make it look so easy and effortless.

The same goes for the way she plays volleyball. I always kept my eye on her when she was on the court. She wasn't the tallest girl in the gym, but she was the most well rounded player who made the biggest impact. She could spike with her left and right hand effectively, and holds school records for digs, aces, kills, and just about any other statistic you can think of.

She ended up being awarded the captain of the all-area volleyball team while I was barely an all-second stringer of the football team. One Friday night after a football game, I stopped and talked to Steph and her friends. One of Steph's friends pulled me aside and said she had a secret to tell me. She said one of her friends wanted to ask me a question. The question was along the lines of "Did you get a speeding ticket today?" I replied, no with a questioned look on my face. "Well, you should have, because you've got *fine* written all over you." It wasn't every day that I got a pick-up line thrown at me, so I just laughed and blushed a little bit.

Her friend went on to urge me to guess who wanted to tell this to me. Only one name came to mind, and I knew it was a shot in the dark, but I thought to myself, maybe, just maybe the biggest dream of my life is about to come true. So I paused for a second after she asked me to guess, and I said, "Steph!?" I tried to say it in a way that made it not so obvious that I had been secretly in love with Steph for the last ten years of my life. I was so excited that this might actually be my chance to tell Steph how much I liked her and there was a ray of hope that she might actually like me back! Her friend waited for a second, and then said, "No, guess again." I was not only embarrassed but also a little disappointed that my guess was wrong.

Steph ran into me so many times after that and every time I thought about saying, "So maybe we should go see a movie or something." But I never worked up enough courage. There were many close calls. I came so close, so many times of calling her up and asking her out. I spent over 13 years having this huge crush, but failed to do anything about it.

Help a Kid in Love

> **HeaRT #8**: Have confidence in yourself

Everyone Liked Her

The reason it never happened related to how beautiful, funny, and perfect she is. If you could meet Steph in person and spend just one day with her you could really see how pretty she is, and find out for yourself how fun it is to be with her. The qualities she possesses actually made her seem a bit intimidating to me when I was younger. Why would an ideal girl such as Steph give me a sliver of a chance? After all, I'm just an average guy in the middle of everything.

Another element of the reason I never worked up enough courage to ask her out was due to the fact that I wasn't the only one who liked everything about her. It was obvious to tell that nearly every guy in my class and just about every other guy in school would have given anything to be that lucky guy to be with Steph.

Not only did every other guy like her, she never had a boyfriend all throughout high school. It was always a mystery to me as to how that was always the case. I always pictured her turning down guys left and right. There was no way I was going to handle that kind of rejection. She would just shoot me down in a split second.

There is just something about her that makes everyone else around attracted to her. She just draws you in with a calm and peaceful demeanor and then puts you out of your misery with the most stunning smile you've ever seen in your life.

> **HeaRT #9**: Eventually, you just have to give in

My Benchmark

Ever since I sat in my chair and stared at Steph in the first grade, I have compared every other girl to her. She is what sets the standard for me. Eventually I had to give my dating requirements some slack because I realized no girl on earth can be everything that Steph is to me. Although I've left out the parts of my life during high school where I actually dated other girls, a part of me was always in love with Steph.

Just having her in my life was enough to have a profound impact on the way I saw other girls. To tell the truth, other girls did eventually get my attention. After a long enough time, the thought of being with Steph became so much of a fantasy that I completely disregarded the possibility of it ever happening.

Eventually, a serious relationship developed between me and another girl. I had finally found something to take my mind off of Steph. This relationship was so serious that I could actually see myself marrying someone other than the pretty blond-haired girl that had put me under her spell at the age of six. I had dated this other girl for about two years. The relationship started during the middle of my junior year in high school. She was just as talented and just as special as Steph, which allowed me to finally stop seeing Steph in every one of my dreams. At this point being with Steph was just a figment of my imagination that would never come true, and besides, now I had something else which was real that I could actually be with and no longer had to go on wishing.

Steph was still single at the time... still holding out for someone special to come along in her life. It was always a mystery to me why she never jumped into a relationship like most of her friends and all the other kids in high school did. I just didn't understand it. It seemed like such a waste that the prettiest and funniest girl in school stayed single the entire time.

Towards the end of our senior year, Steph and I were crowned king and queen of sports at Mead High School. Every year our school holds an athletic banquet and awards are given at the end of the ceremony to the voted male and female athletic achievers. It was a pretty good feeling, not the athletic award, but the split-second thought of being a pair with Steph. She could be the queen of my kingdom on any day of the week! I was thinking to myself, "This is the closest she will ever let me call her queen of anything in my life." But it was still fun to pretend that for a moment that she was queen and I was king.

Off to College

After high school, Steph decided to accept an athletic scholarship to play softball at a college that was more than two hours from home. She seemed to have no problem with packing her bags and leaving the friendly comforts of our small town in Nebraska. I on the other hand was a little bit attached, and decided to move an entire two blocks away from my parents' house and attend a nearby community college. It wasn't that I was scared to make a drastic change in my life, or that I was afraid to go to a larger university, but rather, I had always believed that if something isn't broken, why bother trying to fix it. My life at the time was going just fine, and I was really happy. I felt no need to go off to a far away college.

Besides, I had a healthy relationship that was still going strong. Moving away could have messed it all up, so I had plenty of reasons to stay close to home while Steph wanted to get out and discover something new. Everything had gone very well with my relationship with the girl I had dated all through my junior and senior year of high school. We were so comfortable being around each other and got along so well that it just felt like I would be with her forever, just like my parents. It was the first time in my life I was able to see a realistic future with one girl.

> **HeaRT #10**: If it's on your mind, talk to each other about visions of the future

Some People Change

How drastically the first year of college changes things. The relationship that was once going so well started to turn sour. Gradually this girl started showing less interest and spending less and less time with me. The fun and excitement of being a new college student became more important than hanging out with the same lame boyfriend she had during high school. It went from hanging out everyday together, to every other day, to once a week, to only talking once a week. At the rate things were going, I would become old news in a matter of months.

Our relationship was slowly but surely slipping away. I tried so hard to keep the last string from breaking as I could sense it falling apart. I was trying to do anything I could to make it work. Calling her up, telling her how much I cared about her, being extra nice, sending an extra email here or there, and whatever else I could think of that could put the relationship back on the right track. Nothing seemed to budge.

It was such a lonely feeling after being the center of attention and affection for so long. I was finally in a real relationship with a girl that was good enough to take the place of Steph, but now it was gradually fading away. I no longer had someone to count on to hang out with and talk to.

I tried to see it her way. At the time I understood how important friends were and I respected her decision and convinced myself that it would be best to give her space. When in times of doubt, my parents' method of being patient and continuing to love is the route I always take. No demands were made on my part that I should be getting more attention. I didn't throw a fit and didn't get too upset, but the fear of it completely falling apart was still there. For almost two years I had gotten used to being a couple and doing what couples do. But now I was starting to feel alone.

One night one of my friends was having a party so I decided to go, even though I didn't have a date. I wasn't sure who was going to be there, but I figured, "Why not?" Hanging out with my friends would be much better than sitting around at home wishing I could find a way to fix my broken relationship.

> **HeaRT #11**: If they want space, give it to them. But use the space for your own good too

At the party, the usual group of friends was there. It wasn't anything out of the ordinary for a Saturday night. It was good to get out of the house and get my mind off of what wasn't going right with my girlfriend at the time. My friends are the best in the world and never fail to get my mind off of what's bugging me. Somehow they always pull through and get me in a fun mood without ever having to ask me what's wrong.

But that night something else happened that made me feel better. As I was sitting around talking to all of my friends, being the goofball I usually am, I heard a voice and a laugh that I could recognize anywhere. It had been a long time since I heard that laugh and that voice, but immediately, I knew a pretty girl with bleach blond hair just walked in the door. Someone with a down-to-earth mentality, naturally nice demeanor, and happy-go-lucky attitude was there and everyone was glad to see her.

When Steph walked in the door with her friends, everyone's attention immediately turned to her. I first saw her light up the room in the first grade, and 13 years later she was still doing the same thing. It was almost grade school all over again. Everyone noticed Steph. And there I was, immediately reminded of the crush I had on her for so long. But this time it was different. The attraction was still there, but now I had a relationship of my own to worry about, and I wasn't about to give up on it yet.

It was so nice to talk to Steph. I missed her, as a friend, since she had moved away to college and it was nice to catch up with how everything was going. Quite a few of our classmates were there that night, so we all had fun talking and just hanging out as friends. The same big smile was back in the room, and my closely knit group of friends felt whole again now that Steph was back. She only stuck around for a few hours, but it was enough to make me glad I decided not to stay home that night.

It would have been so easy to fall in love with Steph all over again after seeing her that night. But when I went home, for the first time in my life, I saw Steph as just a friend.

The feeling of having a huge crush on her had subsided in the way of just being a friend from high school. And as far as the relationship I was trying to fix was concerned, that did not have quite as much of a positive outlook.

The next few months it continued to get worse. When she couldn't make time for our two year anniversary, I knew something was wrong. I brought up my concerns just enough times to let her know we needed to do something before it all fell apart. She just shrugged me off saying things along the lines about how she's only going to get one chance to be a freshman in college and she needed to spend all of her time with her friends right now.

Gullible as I was, I believed her and agreed with her that she should be spending as much time with her friends as possible. I only became more naïve as time crawled along. She also happened to be a very talented athlete, and she was starting her track season. Not only was she spending more time with her friends, she also required more time to focus on her running. Friends and sports, those were two things I had absolutely no problem letting her focus her time and efforts on instead of me. I could wait until she was done. But then she started hanging around with one of the guys from the track team. I had always trusted her, and always will, and at the time she made it clear that he was just a friend and nothing more.

The time continued to crawl along and soon enough I had to call her up every now and then just to remind her that I was still around and still wanted to see her every once in awhile. But she just didn't seem to care about me. Then one day when we actually found time to be together she was acting really weird, so finally I asked her what was wrong.

Help a Kid in Love

"Chris, there's something I really need to tell you."

When someone says the words, "there's something I really need to tell you," it means one of two things. I have great news for you... or, I have some horrible, horrible news for you. When she finally worked up enough courage to tell me what she needed to say, it was anything but good news.

Come to find out, after I had been so patient, and given her all the space she asked for, the friend from the track team turned out to be more than a friend. She was so disappointed in herself that she let it happen. I knew she meant well, and knew she never meant to do something like that to me. We always talked about how glad we were that we could trust each other. We both presumed neither one of us would ever be in the situation I was now in of having to respond to the comment, "I kissed some other guy. It just got out of hand and I'm sorry."

I don't care how calm, collected, and controlled you are, but when the girl you've been dating for over two years says something like that, the most obvious reaction is to scream and get mad, which was what I wanted to do. But when in doubt, what would my parents do? That's the motto I try to live by and the answer is always: just keep on loving. So I didn't scream, I didn't flip out, I just kept calm and talked through what we could do to fix it and how we could get through it.

HeaRT #12: Listening is the best option, even in times of peril

---

Having a conversation like this and the instance of almost seeing a two year relationship go down the drain would make you think it would open her eyes and make her see what she was letting slip away. But after our conversation, after I let everything sink in for the both of us, I offered that we should pick up the pieces (granted we just hit a huge speed bump) and keep moving on and use the past as a learning experience. Her response was, "I think I still need more space so I can figure everything out."

Even more space was not what I was expecting to hear, but having complete faith, I let her have her space. Nearly three months went by and she still seemed to be happy having her space. It was coming close to about six months of a long, slow, depressing downward spiral to the end of a relationship. However, I was willing to go through whatever needed to be done to make it work. I was thoroughly convinced that there was nothing that would make me give up and let go. Not even an affair was going to rip this relationship apart. We were high school sweethearts just like my mom and dad, and they had made it! Nothing stopped them, and nothing was going to stop us.

Help a Kid in Love

Chapter 3

Out of the Clear Blue Sky

There was nothing that could get in the way of that relationship. There was nothing that would make me give up and let go. If we could get through this speed bump, we could get through anything the rest of our lives. Well, there might be just *one* thing that could change my mind, but it would take a miracle for that to happen.

My buddy was having his high school graduation party one night, so I called just to check and see if my girlfriend wanted to come with and spend some time with me and my friends. Things were looking up as I got a maybe. A maybe was more than what I had been getting in response for the last six months. I knew some of my friends would be there so it wasn't that big of a deal if she didn't actually show up, but I still wanted her to be there.

The party was a typical graduation party. Family and friends showed up and gathered in the garage. Roast beef sandwiches, watermelon, potato chips, and cake were on the menu, and everyone showed up to congratulate my friend on his graduation. It was the end of spring and I was so glad to see some of my friends who had gone off to other colleges. Many of them I had not seen them since Christmas.

After I ate my food, talked and joked around with my friends for awhile, I called up what was still hopefully my girlfriend at the time to see if she was going to be able to make it. Of course, the maybe turned into a no, and again it would be just another night out with the guys.

> **HeaRT #13**: Friends are a great solution to frustration

I was a little bit disappointed she wasn't able to make it, but I would get over it. Besides, there was some catching up to do with some old friends. As I was catching up and talking with my buddies, everyone sort of stopped and turned to look at who had just shown up. Steph and her friends were making another one of their grand entrances where somehow everyone at the party immediately notices they're there. My friends and I were all happy to see her as she had just finished up her softball season. It had been a long time since any of us had seen or talked to her.

She came over to talk to us, said hi, and started catching up with our lives. I was finally comfortable talking to Steph without being incredibly nervous. It was nice just to be able to talk to her like she was just one of my friends. The attraction was still there, just like her smile, that's something that will never go away. But nonetheless, we were just a few old friends catching up on how everything was going.

As the evening went on and the sun went down, the party moved away from the garage to a bon fire away from the house. It was so relaxing just hanging out with all of my friends. We just sat around the fire talking and laughing the night away. It wasn't quite summer yet, so it started to get chilly as the night went on. The warmth of a seat by the fire had become a premium. Steph was sitting next to me most of the night, and when she had to get up, she made sure that I saved her seat.

"Don't let anyone else take my seat," she said, "and promise me that you'll be here when I get back."

She didn't have to ask. That seat had been saved for her ever since we were 6 years old. But this time the feelings were different. We were just friends now, but it was so nice just to have the time to hang out with her. We sat by the fire and talked and laughed all night long. After awhile Steph got out of her seat next to me and started talking to other people at the party.

Eventually, I had to get up to get something to eat and as I was going to sit back down by the fire I saw Steph just standing alone on the porch. She caught my attention, and said, "come over here and talk to me some more." We just sat there on the porch and talked, and talked, and talked. We were catching up on everything we had missed out on over the last year we had been at different colleges. We talked about our brothers and sisters, about school, about her softball season, and everything else we could think of. The conversation lasted for hours. After awhile we both kind of forgot that there were other people at the party. We were both content on sitting there just talking to one another as friends.

After about two or three hours of just talking and laughing, her friends reminded us that they were there too. It was time for them to go home, but there was a slight problem. They didn't have a ride home. It didn't take me long to offer a solution to that problem! "I've got room in my car!" Good thing I drove out to that party all by myself. There was just

Help a Kid in Love

enough room in my car for Steph and her friends to hitch a ride home. Although it probably seemed suspicious that I was leaving the party with a few gorgeous girls, it was just a friendly gesture.

Steph immediately called the rights to the front seat. "I got shotgun!" The front seat was hers for the taking. It was fitting as we had sat by each other all night long just talking each others ears off. Why not sit next to each other on the way home? After I dropped them all off at her friend's house, they told me thanks for the ride, and I said, "No problem." I didn't think anything of it. It was on my way home and I had plenty of room in my car. I would have done that sort of favor for any one of my friends.

> **HeaRT #14**: Friendly gestures go a long way

A few days after the party, I was finally getting time to spend with my girlfriend. It was about time we were able to start putting the pieces back together. Hopefully things could go back to normal now. We were driving to my apartment and along the way I saw a few of my friends hanging out, including Steph, so I stopped and talked to them. We just stopped to say hi and to see what was going on. One of my friends was there and he was talking to everyone about a party he was having that weekend. His parents were on vacation so it was the perfect chance to throw a party at their place. My girlfriend wouldn't be able to make it because she was doing something with her friends, which was no surprise. Steph and her friends had plans of their own as well. They mentioned that they couldn't make it because they were going to a concert.

So here we go again, another party to go to by myself, even though I was supposedly "in a relationship." Although things were beginning to turn around, they were far from perfect. I had almost gotten used to it by that time. Even though it stunk feeling like I was stuck in a situation that I would just have to wait out, it was something I thought we could still get through with patience.

Little did I know that my entire life was about to change that Friday night. That weekend at my friend's house something unexpected happened to me. Something so huge, something so drastic, something so sweet, something so exciting was going to happen to me, and I didn't have the slightest clue that it was about to hit me.

Sometime after about ten o'clock, that mysterious something hit me like a freight train. What could be so exciting, so drastic, so huge, and so sweet, and what has the power and force of a freight train? My tiny, little cell phone rang and it was Steph on the line. She was at her concert and she just felt like giving me a call. It was good to hear from her, and just like the night we were sitting by the bon fire we just started talking away like two best friends. But then my phone started to cut out. My friend lived out in the country so cell phone reception was spotty. Eventually my phone cut out for good. We were having such a good conversation too! A few minutes later, my friend comes up to me and says he's got somebody on his phone that wants to talk to me. Now who's calling me? It was Steph again. She must really have something she wants to tell me if she had the persistence to call back on my friend's phone. Once I got on the line she says there's something that she should just get off her mind.

"Chris, there's something I really need to tell you."

There's something I really need to tell you, those words sounded so familiar for some odd reason. The last time I heard those words was when I found out my girlfriend had been sneaking around behind my back. But maybe this time it was good news I was about to hear, maybe the "something she really had to tell me" was something that I actually wanted to hear.

She stumbled on her words a little bit before she finally got out what she was trying to say, but the words that followed were the sweetest and most fulfilling words that have ever been spoken to me. It was something I had been waiting to hear for a long, long, long time.

Chris Miller

"I think I like you more than a friend.
Actually, I've had a crush on you ever since we were little."

Those words practically paralyzed me for a brief moment. My brain stopped thinking and my heart stopped beating. It took over 13 total years, and 1 year of being 120 miles apart for those words to finally come out. And I'm ashamed that I wasn't the one who spoke up first. But, at that moment, after I heard those words, my entire life just elevated to an entirely different level. It changed EVERYTHING!

> **HeaRT #15**: A few small words can have one incredibly large impact

It took a few seconds for me to respond to what she had just said. "…No way! Are you serious? So have I! Oh my gosh, I can't believe you just said that! Are you sure you just said what you said? Did I hear you right? I can't believe neither one of us has said anything this whole time!" It took a few minutes to get over the shock and excitement of what we both discovered, and a few seconds for me to realize I was rambling, but like best friends we just kept talking away and laughing. If our cell phone batteries would have lasted long enough and if the human body didn't have to sleep, I think that conversation could have lasted forever.

It is such a mystery that I had managed to wait patiently over 13 years to finally tell Steph how I felt about her. When it comes to most things, patience is hard for me to find. Somehow I managed to hold back for all those years. Many people say, "Good things come to those who wait." Based on my experience with Steph, I can conclude that every single person to walk the face of the earth who has uttered those words is right a million times over.

I would like to meet every individual who has ever won the lottery, every winner of the Publisher's Clearing House, and every guy who has ever popped the question to his future wife. If I could talk to every person on earth who has ever received any type of good news, I would argue that the way I felt when Steph made that life-changing phone call was better than anything anyone has ever felt.

Although I was on the verge of running away with the greatest opportunity life had ever placed on my doorstep, I was still faced with a tough decision. My relationship that I was working so hard to keep together was finally starting to come around. And now, the *one* thing that could make me move on and try something new had just said the *one* thing to me that I always thought would take a miracle to be spoken.

My high school girlfriend was finally starting to realize what we had and we were finally on our way to being a normal, happy couple again. But now I had to make the decision of whom to let down, and whose heart to break. No matter what I did, someone was going to get hurt. A choice had to be made between the girl that says she's had a crush on me since grade school and the girl that has dated me the last two years. This is a tough situation to be in, but I can say from experience, let your heart lead the way and you will have no regrets in the future.

Carpe Diem

"But if you listen real close, you can hear them whisper their legacy to you. Go on, lean in. Listen, you hear it? — Carpe... — hear it? — Carpe..., carpe diem, seize the day boys, make your lives extraordinary."

- Dead Poet's Society 1989

There are two Latin phrases which act as guiding beacons to my life. One, is *Carpe Diem*, which means, "Seize the day!" Another is *Memento Mori* which means, "Remember you are mortal."

Now that I knew Steph had liked me for so long, my life would not be complete without finding out what would happen if I seized the day and took a chance with her. Memento Mori! I thought to myself. To the best of my knowledge I get one shot in this life. If an opportunity as big as Steph is sitting at my doorstep, I sure am not going to balk at the occasion. She had stayed single this whole time and now she was ready to finally start dating someone special. How on earth I got to be that special someone I do not know, but it would be impossible for me to turn down that chance.

> **HeaRT #16**: There are times to be rational, and times to take chances; when in doubt, follow your heart

Although it was already made up in my mind what I wanted to do, and could already feel what the right thing to do was, it was still difficult to actually take action and do what needed to be done. A line from the movie Braveheart was just enough to push me over the edge. If you have yet to see the movie Braveheart I urge you to do so. It is a masterpiece of a story about Scotland's national hero William Wallace. It's easy for me to relate to him as he too reunited with his childhood love.

Although I am at the opposite end of the hero spectrum when compared to William Wallace, there is much to be learned from him. In one of my favorite scenes, William has a dream that he is lying on a bed next to his father who has died in battle. His father's cold dead body turns its head and whispers to William,

"Your heart is free, have the courage to follow it."

Every time I watch the movie, this scene has an electrocuting effect that sends a chill down my spine. To me, there are no other words more powerful, motivating, and inspiring than, "Your heart is free, have the courage to follow it."

Making the decision to take a chance on Steph was something that I knew I had to do even though it meant I would have to break someone else's heart. My most sincere and straightforward attempt was made to break the news to my girlfriend lightly. I told her that I would be open and honest with any questions she had and would always be willing to talk to her whenever she wanted. But she was crushed. Telling her that I was moving on was one of the hardest things

I've ever had to do. Even though it was tough, I knew there was something else great waiting to happen in my life.

> **HeaRT #17**: Use honesty and empathy when you have to tell someone bad news

The Start of Something Good

As soon as I took care of everything required to move on, Steph and I went away talking again about how odd it was that it all ended up this way. What were the chances? What took so long? It really didn't matter how it happened and what took so long, all that mattered was that it finally did happen. Once we got past all the excitement and the emotions, we had to stop and think about what we should do now. We both had the feeling that it would be wrong to rush into something as I had just gotten out of a serious relationship. I agreed with her that it would be best to take it slow and try not to do anything irrational.

We talked on the phone and hung out with each other every night that summer ever since she changed my life with her phone call. One night when we were talking on the phone, she made me listen to a certain song. It's called Follow Through, by Gavin Degraw. She urged me to listen to the song, and more specifically she said, "You have to listen to the words." It was her subtle way of telling me, "I'm serious about being with you, but you have to come through on your end of the bargain." After I listened to the song, I told her that

I loved the song, which was my subtle way of telling her, "There is nothing you have to worry about." Follow Through became our special song, and I was subtly promising her that I would always follow through in our relationship.

> **HeaRT #18**: Before jumping into anything, get on the same page and communicate your expectations

Help a Kid in Love

Follow Through

Oh, this is the start of something good
Don't you agree?
I haven't felt like this in so many moons
You know what I mean?

And we can build through this destruction
As we are standing on our feet
So since you want to be with me
You'll have to follow through
With every word you say
And I, all I really want is you
For you to stick around
I'll see you everyday
But you have to follow through
You have to follow through

These reeling emotions they just keep me alive
They keep me in tune
Oh, look what I'm holding here in my fire
This is for you
Am I too obvious to preach it?
You're so hypnotic on my heart
So since you want to be with me
You'll have to follow through
With every word you say

Chris Miller

The words you say to me
are unlike anything
That's ever been said
And what you do to me
is unlike anything
That's ever been

Am I too obvious to preach it?
You're so hypnotic on my heart
So since you want to be with me
You'll have to follow through
With every word you say
And I, all I really want is you
For you to stick around
I'll see you everyday

So since you want to be with me
You'll have to follow through
I'll see you everyday
But you have to follow through
You have to follow through
You're gonna have to follow

Oh, this is the start of something good
Don't you agree?

The Longest Three Weeks of my Life

We were both on common terms that it was up to me to follow through and make sure I treated her right. With Steph, following through would be a natural reaction and a walk in the park for me. She also brought up the idea that we should wait exactly three weeks before becoming more than friends, just to make sure we weren't moving too fast or jumping into something we thought might be a mistake. I agreed to her terms, although I felt it was unnecessary. I was so sure she was everything I had ever wanted. Granted, a drastic change had just been made to be with her, but still, this was what I had always wanted.

One night she had stayed at my place to hang out and watch a movie with me. When it was time for her to go home, we started the habit of taking the longest time to say goodnight. We would just stand outside and talk, and talk, and talk. She was always in such a happy-go-lucky mood and would always just smile through the entire conversation. When you talk to her you can do nothing but smile back. Her cheerful demeanor is intoxicating and contagious.

> **HeaRT #19**: Common sense should be of the essence, as sometimes we tend to run away with emotions

After that night it was time to walk her to her car and tell her good night. It had been three days, not three weeks, but I felt like I waited long enough. After I said goodnight, I was thinking to myself, "Carpe Diem, seize the day," and I tried to kiss her good night. Notice I said "tried." How embarrassing! She really meant it when she said *three* weeks. Well, now I know, when a woman says, "Let's wait," she really means it.

During part of our relationship preparation stage, we started talking about how so many times people get involved in relationships and they end up ruining the friendship that led to the relationship. We both noted how unfortunate it was that this happens, so we made a pact. Actually, it was a pinky swear. We pinky swore that no matter what, no matter how good or bad things ended up, no matter what happened tomorrow or all the days after that, we would always be friends. Friendship has always been the most important thing to both of us. I had a feeling we would never have to worry about what would happen if things didn't work out. It was simple. Things would just always work out. How could they not? But we still took the time to insure our friendship by paying the premium of a pinky swear.

> **HeaRT #20**: Focus on friendship and make it a priority, as it is the glue that holds it all together

We made the pinky swear on day four. I had 17 more days to go for the three weeks to finally be over. Those three weeks were an eternity for me. We both knew we wanted to be more than friends, but she was disciplined enough to wait and I couldn't help myself. Maybe she thought there was a chance one of us would back out during those three weeks. I knew I wasn't going to. I just couldn't wait for those three weeks to end.

Help a Kid in Love

Chapter 4

She's the One

I'll never forget the night we put an end to our three week waiting period. We were hanging out with our friends one night and were on our way to a low-key live concert at one of the local bars. After the concert we were going to stay the night at her friend's house.

At the concert everything was perfect. The music, the lights, the people, the weather, and the timing all seemed like the perfect night. As I say concert, you have to think about it from a small-town, Nebraska perspective. It was really just a glorified outdoor bar party with the addition of a live band. But the size of the event had nothing to do with the magnitude of our attraction. We were glued to each other. It was a different feeling I had never felt before, and I didn't know exactly how to act or what to say being on the frontier of becoming more than friends with the girl I had dreamed about being with for more than two thirds of my entire life. As awkward as it might have been, I would be willing to go through that feeling over and over again if I could.

After the singing, dancing, and socializing took its toll, we worked our way through the bar on our way home. The place was packed. It was so crowded that the only way you could move was by pushing your way through the crowd. Steph and I eventually pushed our way to an open part of the room, and she was leaning up against a wall with the most innocent and tantalizing look on her face. She gives me another one of her heart-piercing smiles and says, "I really want to kiss you right now, I wish I wouldn't have told you we have to wait." How dare she say that! It was pure torture!

Eventually we made our way out of that crowded bar and went back to her friend's house. It was me and Steph, and two of our friends that would be staying the night and sleeping in the same basement. It was a wide open basement and we were just sleeping on blankets and pillows right on the floor. Our relationship was still new at the time and our friends were still under the impression we were just "real good friends" so we didn't want things to seem awkward or out of place so I arranged my blanket and pillow on the opposite side of the room as she had.

That night was perfect. I even remember the date; June 26th, 2004. It was technically within the three week waiting period, but again, my impatient self decided it was close enough. I waited another eternity for our friends to fall asleep. Once I waited long enough, and made sure they were sound asleep, I picked up my pillow and blanket and crawled my way in the pitch black basement to where Steph was laying. She was still awake, still up, still waiting for me to come and talk to her. We whispered back and forth about how we couldn't believe we were finally together. I told her how she always caught my attention, how I always thought she looked so cute, and that she's always been the girl of my dreams. It made her blush and all she could say was, "you always know exactly what to say."

Eventually I couldn't take it anymore. This was too perfect, the time just seemed so right. So I finally made my second attempt at our first kiss. Again it was breaking the three week rule of waiting, but I couldn't wait any longer. Not only had we waited the last two and a half weeks, we had also waited more than a decade for this moment to happen. I just could not wait.

> **HeaRT #21**: Savor the sensation of the first kiss

And neither could she! After waiting all this time, and holding back for so long we made up for lost time. It was nothing short of amazing. How do you describe a kiss with words? Mostly, all I can say is that it was flawless. She kisses in a way that makes you forget where you're at and makes you feel dizzy and lost. It's a feeling that puts you in another world, and all you can sense around you is her. Nothing else in the world exists at that moment. Everything just seems to vanish and float away. It gave me goosebumps, sent shivers up my spine, and made my heart race on overdrive. In short, it was breath-taking, mushy, warm, moist, juicy, tender, luscious, succulent, magnetizing, heart-throbbing, wonderful, astonishing, mind-blowing, silky smooth, addictive, memorable…. and above all, perfect.

When you are in love with someone for so long and finally get a chance to kiss them, all your senses in the rest of your body completely evaporate and all you can feel are her lips against yours. You get light-headed and your entire body feels like it could just float away. Your toes curl and your skin tingles. Your eyes have nothing better to do than close. If they were open they wouldn't function anyways as the brain is too busy computing the incredible signals the lips are sending it.

Something about that kiss was different than anything else I've ever experienced in my life. It made me lose track of time, lose track of where I was and made me lose all sense of feeling in my entire body. When we were finally through, we both realized we weren't in the same spot anymore. It was kind of like we just magically floated to a different place on the floor. I don't think either one of us realized which direction we ended up facing. I tried to get up to figure out where the stairs were, but had no clue anymore which way was which. I had literally gotten lost in her kiss. We both were dumbfounded that we didn't know who or what was where. We were lost in each other too long and didn't know what way to go.

That Summer

That wasn't the only amazing time we kissed that summer. Every kiss after that was just as amazing and made me feel just as lost. We had our way of taking our sweet time kissing each other good night. We always had to have just a little bit more of each other before saying the last goodnight. I would walk out the door and she would close it halfway, and then I'd step back in for just a few more minutes of bliss.

During the first few months of our relationship we were both so far under the influence, in some sort of synchronized stumble of love. We talked about how we shouldn't expect anything for certain to happen in the future.

We took the moment and ran with it without looking back or fretting about the future. "I can't promise you what's going to happen from here," she said. My instant reply was, "It doesn't matter. This has all been worth it so far." We both knew that the future held no promises, but we were also so glad to be in the same present moment of amazement and affection.

> **HeaRT #22**: At the start, ease the pressure by having no expectations and just enjoy the moment

    Most of the time that summer she came to visit me at my apartment which was the central meeting place. All of our friends knew they were always welcome. The rule was that you don't knock on the door when you come into my apartment, you just walk in! My place was where everyone came to meet when there was nothing to do, and was where everyone came for most big occasions. One night I'll always remember was on the weekend of Mead Days. Once a year, our small little town turns into one giant carnival, one big celebration, and often generates unforgettable memories. This year was no exception.

    All of our friends were at my apartment hanging out, waiting for the fireworks to get underway. The plan was that we were all going to walk up to the park which was just a few blocks away. As the sun went down, we all decided we should make our way to the park to get some good seats for the show. It was cloudy and cool that night for a Nebraska summer, so I made sure to grab a jacket and to make sure

Steph was warm. With her by my side, and our friends in front of us we began the two block trek.

It's funny how strange some of the things me and Steph had in common. That night we both realized we were a pair of the slowest walkers on the planet. Our friends in front of us seemed to gradually get farther and farther from us. After a while we'd have to jog to catch up with them. We just liked to take our sweet time. About halfway to the park a few sprinkles started falling from the sky. The rain didn't bother our friends, but it gave us an excuse to go back to the apartment to get something to shield ourselves from the rain. I said that we'd better get something to get Steph out of the rain. "As sweet as she is, she might melt!"

> **HeaRT #23**: Even if it's corny, never pass up the chance to compliment your special someone

We went back to grab a blanket to put over our heads. With the makeshift umbrella above us, we were back on our way to the park and were now taking a shortcut, and just as we got to the apartment garages the first of the fireworks went off. We could have kept walking to catch up with our friends, but instead we just stopped to find our own little world next to the garage. There was just enough awning overhead to keep us out of the rain, and we still had a decent view of the fireworks. It was another perfect moment to get lost again. A cool summer night, with the soundtrack of rainfall, the background of fireworks, and one incredibly cute girl was resting in my arms is one scene that I'll never forget from my life. It was another perfect moment for her to make me feel dizzy.

It wasn't the fireworks, it wasn't the rain, it wasn't the time of the night, or the cool breeze in the air that made it so perfect. It was the way she looked and the way she kissed that made my knees weak. The sweet innocent kisses she gave me felt much like the cool sprinkles falling from the sky that night. Half of the time we were in awe of the beautiful fireworks, and the other half we were simply in awe of each other. The fireworks show was nothing short of spectacular, but paled in comparison to the beauty of my memory of just being with her that night.

For the rest of that summer, we always found time to be lazy. We both were working summer jobs, so any time we spent together, we used strictly for rest, relaxation, and affection. Whether we were just sitting inside on the couch watching television together, going out to eat and catching a movie, or lounging by the pool we were thrilled to be around each other even if there wasn't anything to do.

We both savored and enjoyed every second together that summer. We didn't talk about it much, but we both knew that we wouldn't get the opportunity to be together nearly as much as soon as school started. We both knew it would be different being separated by more than a hundred miles. We just enjoyed every second together and always made the most out of our time. And when it was time to say good night, those seconds were stretched as far as possible.

Time for School

Although we did everything we could to make that summer last forever, the day came when Steph had to pack up her car and move back into her dorm, which was 120 miles from my apartment. According to Mapquest, it takes roughly 2 and a half hours to get from my apartment to Steph's dorm. But it depends on how fast you drive, or in my case, how deeply in love you are. The time it takes to get from Mead, Nebraska to Steph's dorm can drastically be reduced when you know she is there waiting for you.

We thought it would be tough adjusting to the distance, but the relocation actually added a little bit of excitement and anticipation to the relationship. I remember the first time I drove up to see her. Although I shaved off some time of the trip with my lead foot, the drive still seemed like it took forever. During the summer it took a whole ten minutes to get to Steph, now it took an eternity.

But the drive was more than worth it when I finally got to her dorm. After a two hour car ride, there's nothing like the view of a gorgeous blond girl, standing outside, wearing her dazzling smile as usual, just waiting to give you a big hug. "You made it, I'm so glad to see you!" She said she would give me a tour of campus as soon as I dropped off some of my stuff in her room. It had been awhile since we last saw each other, and I was thinking about nothing but her for the entire two hour car ride. As soon as she shut the door to her dorm room I got lost again. Just to give you an idea of what the most amazing kiss in the world is like, you can get a fraction of the feeling if you spin around in circles really fast for about

30 seconds in one spot and then stop, close your eyes and lick your lips real slow. It will give you a very tiny fraction of what the real thing feels like.

That day we started the weekly tradition of being the biggest bums in her dorm room. Driving all that way to see her and having nothing in particular to do when I got there was better than any vacation I've ever taken. Each week it was like a little getaway for me. Besides school, I worked a full time schedule, so it was so calm and relaxing just to lie around her dorm room for the entire day. Being lazy was our way of milking the time we had to together. If we just lay around and do nothing, maybe we could make time just crawl along. Being able to slow down time was much too difficult because we always had so much fun. It's amazing how two people stuck in an eight by ten foot cramped dorm room can stay entertained for an entire day. After being as lazy as possible we would eventually get up and do something. We would go for walks, grab a bite to eat, check out what was happening on campus, get some exercise, and hang out with her friends.

Steph is not a shy person by any means, but when compared to her friends she seems very conservative. Her friends are not afraid to do whatever it takes to make you laugh and are always looking for a good time. We all got along great, even though for the longest time I was only known as "Bergie's boyfriend." It was always so easy to get along with each other's friends and there were never any issues of balancing the time between our friends and time spent alone with each other. We just went with the flow and never had a problem.

> **HeaRT #24**: Make time to spend with each other's friends, but carve out some alone time as well

The Passenger Seat

Every time I went up to see her we always found a way to set aside some time to go on a date. Whether we were going to a movie, a dinner at a nice restaurant, or a trip to the mall, I think the most amazing time we spent together was in the car on the way to wherever it was we were going. In the car anything would fly. We would sing along to the radio, and just be absolute goofballs. One of Steph's favorite bands is SheDaisy. They sing a song called "Passenger Seat" that has a few lines we may have took a little too literally.

"Life's so sweet right here in the passenger seat. Can't imagine a moment any better than this… Then we kiss."

Whenever we were in my car, Steph would be sitting next to me in the passenger seat and we would always throw looks back and forth as I was trying to drive. She would kick off her sandals or shoes and put her feet under her and sit up real tall in her seat and would sit as close to me as she could. And I would always lean over just a little bit in my seat while I was driving. We'd get real close so we could sing and joke right in each other's face. We'd get so carried away and start laughing at each other, and eventually we would wind up kissing again.

But now we weren't in a dorm room and not in a basement, we were driving on the highway! Out of the corner of my eye, I could barely see the road ahead of us as my head was turned to the middle of the car. Just being around Steph was enough to get my adrenaline going, but now we were in a car going 60 miles an hour! We were just two crazy kids in love. Kissing in a car on the highway is probably more dangerous than drunk driving. It sure is more intoxicating.

> **HeaRT #25**: Do not try this at home!

When we'd finally stop to focus on not getting in an accident she would just start laughing and I would fall back to the middle of my seat, partly to catch my breath from almost putting my car in the ditch, and another part of exhaling from another amazing kiss. It's kind of like when you're really thirsty and you drink an ice cold glass of water. When you're done it makes you say "ahhhhhh." When I'd slide back into the driver's seat I'd always quietly say under my breath, "ahhhhh, that was amazing."

Care-Free Attitude

Doing spontaneous things like kissing in the car on the middle of the highway was a common occurrence when we were together. You never knew what was going to happen. She would never fail to come out of nowhere to make a face or say something that could keep me laughing for days. Besides saying the most random things, she never failed at making a funny face at the most opportune time or cracking a smile when you thought she was getting really upset and serious.

Whenever we met each other at a public place she would just flash her big smile and would give me her bobble-head doll wave. We had the funniest way of waving at each other. At one of her brother's basketball games she noticed one of the players from the opposing teams had a hilarious way of playing defense. He would come charging towards the baseline with his hands held up high and his head bobbing from side to side. She thought it was so funny how he looked like a bobble-head doll that she decided to wave at people the same way. She'd put her hands up above her shoulders shaking them from side to side with her head bobbing in the opposite direction. Whenever we saw each other, that's how we waved and it never failed to get both of us cracking up.

> **HeaRT #26**: If you're not willing to make a complete fool of yourself, you don't deserve to be in love

She can entertain you in person just as easily as she can over the phone. Six days of the week while school was in session our relationship resided over the phone. We talked on the phone every night and we would talk about how our day went, and about how we couldn't wait to see each other. We would talk and talk for hours. Eventually we would run out of things to talk about. I'd always end up saying, "I got nothing." And that was about the time we would just start making up stories. We couldn't get enough of each other's voice that we would just start telling each other fictional stories made up on the spot. If we would have recorded them all we probably could have published an entire book of funny short stories. One of the best ones she told was about the ladybug named Lady that was living in my apartment. I don't have to tell you anything about the story to make my point that we were just talking for talking sake so we could hear each other's voice. It didn't even have to make sense. It just had to be audible.

"Happy-go-lucky" comes close to describe her attitude. I've never met another person who is able to let it all loose, but at the same time has the self-respect and intelligence not to let it go too far. She's a deadly combination of a girl with a free-spirit, fun-loving mind-set with a level of poise and discipline that makes you sit and wonder how she pulls it all off. All you can do is fall in love with her.

> **HeaRT #27**: Love is what makes you feel young and free, but is not an excuse to be irresponsible and immature

Kissable, Huggable, Loveable, Unbelievable!

I can't remember exactly where we were or exactly what we were doing, but one day I just started telling her that she is just so kissable. And then I told her she's so huggable too. And the list kept going on and on about how she's just so loveable and altogether unbelievable. At the time I said it, the thought hadn't crossed my mind, but the words I was telling her were already in the form of a song.

Help a Kid in Love

A few days after I told her how kissable, huggable, and unbelievable she was, we were driving in her car and a song came on the radio that I believe was written specifically about her. When it came on, we both started singing it, and about halfway through the song we looked at each other and both started laughing because I had said almost the exact same things a few days before we ever heard the song together. I said, "They wrote this song about you!" She laughed, and at the same time seemed to silently agree with me. Just like her attitude, it's a fun, upbeat song, and part of it goes like this:

She's so kissable...
huggable... lovable... unbelievable...

She's a mouthful of anything
and everything a man could want

She ain't typical, she's unpredictable,
she's available, it's a miracle

How my heart stumbled into someone so
kissable, huggable, lovable, unbelievable

Up 'til now my life has been so lonely....
and boring....

I never thought I would find someone so...

Elegant, intelligent, heaven sent
all my money spent

She's so beautiful, it's indisputable, it's
undeniable, she's gotta-havable

*She's music to my ears, and makes my heart
sing, so kissable, huggable, lovable,
unbelievable*

Whew...

Whenever that song came on the radio we would sing it from the top of our lungs and just die laughing because it was so true. At the end of the song we would always let out the big sigh of, Whew! If you ever listen to the song (it's by Diamond Rio) you'll understand the last part of the song as it goes by so fast that by the end of the song you've got to stop and take a breath which is the same way I felt anytime I was around Steph. Once you finally part with Steph for the night and say the very last goodbye, you have to stop and take a breath and just say, "Whew!"

Softball Season

After we had so much fun hanging out, and after I got used to making the 4 hour round trip once a week to hang out with her all day long, and after we got used to talking on the phone every night, we eventually had to cut back on how much we saw of each other as softball season got underway. She traveled often for road games and always had practice on the days I was able to come up to see her so we had to get used to keeping in touch whenever we could find small amounts of time to chat on the phone.

Help a Kid in Love

There was a stretch of about three weeks where we were both so busy that we couldn't find time to hang out. Three weeks might not sound too bad for some people being apart, but for us it was an eternity. We just couldn't wait that long. But there just wasn't any free time, and it was too far away to make a quick trip to hang out.

Finally I couldn't take it anymore. I called her on my way home from work one afternoon, and asked what she was planning on doing that night. She said she would just be hanging out with one of her friends. By that time it was about five o'clock and it was a Thursday night. She had class the next morning and I had to work so it was turning into another conversation which would likely end in, "hopefully I get to see you sometime soon."

> **HeaRT #28**: Take some chances and do the unexpected

After we got off the phone, I hopped in my car, and took off for her dorm. I missed her way too much. By the time I got to her dorm room it was around seven o'clock and I called her and asked if she wanted to hang out with me since I was in town. "You're where!?" She was so shocked and ecstatic to see me there. Although I drove a round-trip total of four hours, I only got to stay three, but it was all worth it just to see her smile when I showed up to surprise her.

Back at Home Again

Getting through the end of the spring semester and all the way through her busy softball schedule was tough, but it only made the upcoming summer that much more enjoyable. Finally we were able to see each other more than once a week. She was back at home for the summer and I was thrilled I could now drive just a few minutes (not hours) to be able to see her. Even though we were used to seeing each other only once a week, as soon as she was back for the summer we made sure we saw each other at almost every possible opportunity. She worked in town so on my days off I would always make lunch for her. And as soon as she got off work in the evening she'd call me and we'd be together in a matter of minutes.

That summer we spent a great deal of our time in her pool at her house. I'm not the type of guy that likes to swim, and being lazy is something I actually have to practice at, but with Steph everything seems to naturally relax. Just being able to lounge around in the sun and just being a bum was something I never took the time to do on my own. Being with her was therapeutic for my busy and hectic work schedule. Besides working full time, I also took summer classes so the lazy days I spent with Steph were like heaven on earth.

Never before have I actually sat out and tanned, but somehow, with Steph, it was able to happen that summer. She taught me how to actually sit still for awhile and just soak up the sun. As long as she was by my side I had no problem not doing anything besides enjoying the moment. After we had enough of the sun we would end up taking a nap inside on her couch with the air conditioning on full blast. We would get toasty hot lying outside in the sun, and then would come inside and cuddle up under a blanket. The combination of her sun-warmed body and her silky smooth skin was another one of the most comforting and soothing sensations I've ever experienced, and is a feeling I'll never forget. It was kind of like after you put a really soft blanket in the dryer and as soon as it's done, you take it out and just immerse yourself in the softness and warmth.

      She took incredible care of her skin and it was always amazingly smooth, or "smoove," as we would say. After awhile we started using some of our own made up words that would always make us laugh. Her *smoove* skin was just one of the many things about her that made me melt. Beyond being incredibly personable and intelligent, she is just naturally gorgeous. To top it all off she has a knack for taking meticulous care of herself and also had a knack for fashion always wearing the cutest clothes. There's wasn't a single time that I didn't tell her that she looked cute, and it was never something I was just saying to be nice. It was always the truth. She was always stunning and beautiful, inside and out.

      And in a dress, that was a different story. As soon as she puts on a dress, she goes from incredibly cute to completely irresistible. My older sister had her wedding that summer and on her wedding night there was an incredibly beautiful girl in a dress, but it wasn't white and it wasn't my sister. Steph had picked out the perfect dress that just made my jaw drop when I saw her in it. It isn't fair to the rest of the world how gorgeous she is, especially in a dress.

      That night at the wedding reception I could have danced with Steph all night long. My family and most of my friends were there and more than once I heard the comment, "so, next time we'll be at a wedding reception, we'll be toasting Chris and Steph." I just smiled and didn't say anything. What a dream come true that would be. But to tell the truth, the thought of being married never really crossed my mind, and I know up until then Steph had never thought about it much either. We were having too much fun being around each other and enjoyed the moment way too much to even start thinking about the future. The wonderful thing about our relationship was that it simply went day by day. There were never any daunting expectations and we never bothered to worry about what happened in the past, or what might or might not occur in the future.

> **HeaRT #29**: The past is gone, the future will come, just enjoy the present moment

A Dream Come True

Although until this point, the thought of marriage never completely materialized into either one of our minds, it eventually started to feel like we were on our way of being together forever. We got along so well ever since the beginning and never had any problems. We never had a hard time communicating, seemed to do nothing but laugh when we were together, always had something to do, and always got along perfectly. We always found something new and exciting to do together and there was never a single argument. We were in love at the deepest level, but we always found time to be around friends and family. There was not a single thing about our relationship that wasn't working. It had it all.

Besides the fact that we had secret crushes on each other for more than a decade, the things that really made our relationship great was the things that we never knew about each other until we finally started dating. The things that we discovered were perfect compliments. Her free-spirited, carefree attitude was just the thing to balance out my non-stop need to be constantly at work on something. How we walked so slow side by side, kissed so incredibly during the night, and how she could always guess what I had to tell her when I would say, "Steph, Guess What?" And even what we were studying in school were almost perfect yin and yang combinations. She was a therapeutic recreation major learning how to spend the rest of her life happy and healthy while I was a finance major learning how to spend the rest of my life wealthy. There was no way a happy, healthy, and wealthy couple with such a long history would ever part.

> **HeaRT #30**: Realize what you've got, if it's something special, never take it for granted.

Falling in love with Steph made my life complete. If I died today, I would be happy as ever because I got at least one chance to be with the woman of my dreams. Ever since she called me on the phone and said she wanted to be more than my friend, I never took it for granted, not even for a second. She was everything I had ever wanted and more. She is the love of my life, a dream come true, a perfect match, a heaven-sent blessing, kissable, huggable, loveable, and altogether unbelievable. She was always that something special that was waiting to come into my life. She showed me how to take chances. She taught me how to relax. She always made me laugh, and always gave me the most incredible kisses I'll never forget. There was nothing at all that I saw wrong with her and there was not a single thing I would change if I could. It was a miracle she came into my life the way she did and because of her she made all of my dreams come true. Without a doubt...

She's the one...

Help a Kid in Love

She's the One

She's the one in 20 classmates that I dreamed about in school
She's the one in 500 people from our small town that I
couldn't wait to spend the rest of my life with
She's the one in 6.5 billion people on the
face of the earth that has had my name
written all over her heart for the
past 15 years of my life

She's the one who lit up the room and caught my attention first
She's the one who can steal my heart away at any moment
She's the one I would take a chance on again and again
She's the one that will always own a piece of my soul
She's the one which I compare everything else to
She's the one that always makes me smile
She's the one who I always wanted

She's the one that taught me how to enjoy life
She's the one I always have fun being around
She's the one that showed me how to live
She's the one that always made me laugh
She's the one that allowed me to love

Her voice makes my head turn
Her smile makes me give in
Her beauty makes me cry
Her spirit set me free

Chris Miller

She's the one that paralyzed me with words from her mouth
She's the one that made me dizzy by the touch of her lips
She's the one I would travel any distance to be with
She's the one that belongs in my passenger seat

She's the one that made my life complete

She's my one and only,

She's the one…

The one I want the *entire* world to know I love

Help a Kid in Love

Chapter 5

My Treasure, My Proof

Whenever I think of Steph, I think of her as my treasure. She's that most special thing that has made my life worthwhile. She was that one thing that I spent the majority of my life wishing would someday be in my hands. Just like that moment when we were kids and found the clamshell in her pond, we were filled with hope of finding a perfect ivory-white, sparkling pearl on the inside. Since I was six years old I have been filled with hope that someday, just someday, something spectacular would happen where Steph would fall in love with me. And then one day, she made a phone call that changed my life. Ever since that day I knew I had been holding a perfect, sparkling, ivory-white pearl in my hands. Being with her was something I always treasured.

Although she was a treasure in my heart and a pearl in my hands, as the summer was coming to an end I'd have to get used to not seeing her every day. School was about to start back up, and we had to make another adjustment of being two hours away from each other. Last year we got through the nine months of school with no problems. This time we would know what to expect and it wouldn't be long until we were out relaxing in the sun again. She moved out of her cramped dorm room and rented an apartment. I was glad that she upgraded, but part of me was still going to miss spending the entire day in a cramped dorm room with her. As the semester got underway, we were back into the swing of a long distance relationship. But it was no big deal, nothing we couldn't handle.

> **HeaRT #31**: Confidence and faith are what can get you through hard times and sudden adjustments

Biggest Scare of My Life

About a month and half after she had settled into her new apartment she invited me to come up to hang out with her for the weekend. It was the weekend which kicked off the university's homecoming festivities. I was excited to see Steph and hang out with her for the weekend as it had been over a week since either had last been together. After the two hour car ride I finally saw Steph's smiling face waiting for me at her apartment.

The weekend started off feeling just like any other time I had visited Steph. It was Friday evening when I got there, so there was just enough time to stop and grab a bite to eat and then we caught up with her friends. Hanging out with Steph and her friends was nothing new for me. We all got along great and always had a blast together. They were all happy to see us when we showed up and it felt like it would be another fun weekend.

That night we went to a house party across the street from Steph's apartments. Steph spent most of the night talking to her friends. I didn't mind the fact that she was spending more time with her friends as I knew I got more than my fair share of time with her, and there would be more time in the future that we would have for ourselves. So that night it was not a problem that I wasn't the center of attention.

Eventually, Steph and her friends decided they wanted to go downtown to the bars with most of the other girls. They were all 21, so they could just flash their ID's and walk right in. I was a few months away from turning 21 so I said it was ok for them to leave without me. "We won't be too long. We'll come back in a couple of hours," they said.

Three hours went by and there was no phone call and no Steph to be heard of. I tried calling and she didn't answer. She should have been back by that time so I asked a few strangers at the party if they had seen or talked to Steph lately. Some didn't know Steph by her name so I'd have to explain, "She's a pretty blond girl on the softball team who's always in a happy mood and has a really big smile." They'd respond, "oh, I know who you're talking about… no I haven't seen her." By this time it was past midnight so I left a voice mail on Steph's phone to let her know that I would be at her apartment until she came home.

A few more long slow hours dragged on and there was still no Steph. It was almost 2:00 AM and I couldn't take it anymore. I called one last time hoping to hear her voice just to make sure she was alright. Again there was no answer. After she didn't answer I called each one of her friends until I found out she was alright. Eventually I got a hold of someone who assured me that Steph was doing fine. By that time I was more than ready to get some sleep.

The next morning I woke up early even though I hadn't gotten much sleep. I checked the living room to see if Steph had made it home and on her couch in the living room there was a blond-haired girl sound asleep on the couch. The sun hadn't come up completely yet so it was still fairly dark in the room. All I could see was the back of her head which was just enough to wash a feeling of relief over me knowing she was ok. I wasn't about to wake her up, but I started walking closer to the couch to tuck in a blanket for her.

As I started walking closer, I saw something that made my heart jump out of my chest. It shocked me so much that I couldn't even move. Was this a nightmare? This couldn't be real, this couldn't be happening again. Lying right next to Steph was some punk kid that had absolutely no right to be sleeping on the same couch as her. My muscles tightened and a warm rush of blood went all through my body.

Next to the couch was a pair of shoes that belonged to someone who was two seconds away from being awakened with a hard right hook to the jaw. What do you do in a moment like this? How do you react? I just didn't want to believe it. There was no way she would ever do something like this. She is just not the kind of person who would make a mistake like that and go behind my back. She's so much more responsible than this, but I had to do something.

Luckily I was able to keep my cool enough not to hurt anyone before they woke up. I figured the best thing to do would be to wake up Steph first and let her tell me what was going on. So a light tap of the shoulder, and the blond head wiggles a little bit as it was getting an early awakening. She finally turns her head enough to show her face, and come to find out.... IT'S NOT STEPH!!!!! It's one of her friends! They both had the same color and length of hair that was easy to get mixed up especially in a half darkened room. The weight of the world was instantly lifted off of my shoulders and the most horrific thoughts left my mind as quickly as they had entered. It was embarrassing that I woke up her friend when she was on the couch with some guy I didn't know, so I quickly apologized and asked her where Steph was.

> **HeaRT #32**: Don't freak out until you know the facts

Come to find out, Steph was sound asleep (alone) at her friend's apartment. What a relief! Everything was ok. I could breathe again and ignored the fact that some stranger was on the couch with her friend. It was a microscopic issue after being worried about Steph. I went back into Steph's room to go back to sleep and next to her bed on her dresser I noticed her cell phone. She had left it there the entire night. That's why she wasn't answering! Everything was starting to make sense and all my worries of being ignored and cheated on for the second time were gone to the wayside now. Thank goodness!

I slept for a few more hours and after awhile the front door of the apartment started to creak open. It was Steph! She was ok! She was back! She was alive! Her friend and the mysterious guy on her couch were still sound asleep, so as soon as Steph came into the door I had to whisper, "Steph, you have *NO IDEA* how glad I am to see you," which was a tremendous understatement. Steph gave me her smile when she walked in the door that completely erased all of the bad feelings that were still lingering in my stomach from my nightmare of confusion.

After she saw me, she looked on the couch and immediately peeled off the strange guy who was sound asleep. She showed no mercy as she just grabbed his shirt, pulled him off without giving him a chance to see where he was, and in a matter of seconds she gave him the boot to the door. Steph forced him to leave and said that he *had* to get out! That's what friends are for! So much for the awkward feeling of waking up next to a stranger as it only took Steph a few seconds to clean up the mess. After she shut the door his shoes were still sitting on the floor. We all saw them at the same time and just started laughing. "He'll be ok, who needs shoes anyways?"

Come to find out, nothing serious had happened at all between the two on the couch. They had both made it home that night and were up talking before they eventually fell asleep. It was nothing more than a conversation. I told Steph about how it looked like it was her laying on the couch and I almost kicked the living daylights out of the poor guy. She just laughed at me and reassured me that nothing like that would *ever* happen. I told her I knew that, but it just scared the bejeesus out of me when I saw what I saw. The nightmare was over, and in a matter of minutes my emotions went through every realm and every nook and cranny from utter shock to soothing relief.

Chris Miller

Something's Different

After that night, I was ready for things just to go back to normal. No more leaving cell phones at home, no more mix ups of strange people sleeping on the couch, no more surprises, and no more nightmares. Later during the day we all went to watch the football game. I was so glad to be able to sit next to Steph and finally spend some time with her. It had been almost an entire day since I arrived and I had only spent a few minutes with her. At the football game, when we were sitting in the stands there was a sensation I never felt between us. There was this strange feeling like she didn't want to talk to me. Conversations usually happened naturally between us, but for some incredibly odd reason things just seemed different. I didn't think too much of it at the time. She must have just been worn out from the late night and was still behind on her sleep.

After the football game there was more celebrating to do. This time I was hoping Steph and her friends would stick around a little bit longer. Eventually, after a few hours of socializing, it was deja vue all over again. Steph and her friends were ready to hit the bars and it looked like I would be spending another night without them. But this time Steph promised me she would have her phone with her and she promised she would come back after awhile.

After a few long hours of sitting in her apartment by myself, she finally came back with her friends. They stopped for a few minutes, but after a brief moment they all were ready to head back to the bars before closing time. Tomorrow I would be going home and I wanted to make the most of every minute so I offered to walk with Steph downtown, just to spend a little bit of time with her while I was there. I didn't want to be selfish and make her stay with me while all her friends went off somewhere else. That five minute walk was the most quality time I got to spend with her the entire weekend.

As soon as we got to the bar I had to stop at the door where they were checking ID's and turn around and walk back to her apartment. Another two hours slowly dragged by and finally Steph came back to her apartment. Finally we could get some time together and we could just hang out and talk. By the time she made it home she mentioned she was too tired to do anything but sleep.

"I've missed you so much since you've been gone," I said. She didn't say anything back. And when I tried to give her a hug it felt like she didn't want to hug me back. She was just going through the motions it seemed like, and then when it was time for the both of us to go to bed there was no magical, long, succulent kiss good night. Something was out of place. I could feel it. I asked if everything was ok and she said she was just tired. Tired or not, things had never felt so out of place. I went to bed that night not knowing what to think. What could it be? What did I do? What didn't I do? What's wrong? How can I fix it?

> **HeaRT #33**: It won't always be perfect, just speak up and be honest if things don't feel right

The next morning we all eventually woke up and it was time for me and her friend to head back home. The entire weekend had been a disaster. I spent only a few minutes with Steph and once we were finally alone things felt out of place which was something that just never happened. As I was packing up my car, Steph and her friend couldn't stop talking about how much fun they had. They obviously were not in the same place as me that weekend. As I was about to leave I tried to get the usual kiss goodbye, but this time there was no getting lost. She just kind of pecked back at me and gave a half-hearted smile. I waited for a few seconds and then asked, "So, is everything ok?"

"It's nothing," she said, "I'll see you and talk to you more next week when I come home." Usually when we said goodbye, I'd get lost in her kiss. This time, the only feeling of being lost was the lost feeling of everything being out of place. Maybe it was just me, maybe it was just the weekend, and maybe she really was just tired. The only thing for certain, was that I confused and worried.

The Talk

On the way home all I could think about was everything that seemed so out of place. There's no way Steph wouldn't want to kiss me goodnight, there's no way we wouldn't spend *some* time together, there's no way she would not want to hang out with me for just a little bit. It had to be a fluke. But if it wasn't, I'd better do something about it!

The next day I talked to one of her friends to see if there was anything I should know before I talked to Steph. "Did anything happen out of the ordinary over the weekend?

Help a Kid in Love

For some reason things seemed a little bit out of place. She just didn't seem like the same old Steph. Is there something I should be worried about?"

Her friend reassured me that there wasn't anything abnormal she knew of, and that there wasn't anything I should be worried about. "Don't worry. I'm sure everything is ok." It made me feel better for a few minutes. After our conversation I dialed Steph's number and was hoping everything was in fact *ok*. When Steph's voice came on the phone I wasn't sure what to say, or if I should bring up what had been bugging me, so I just went ahead talking to her like we always had. Towards the end of the phone call I finally asked if she was sure that there wasn't anything on her mind that she needed to talk about. She said everything was fine and she would see me in a few days when she came home. She was coming back home to her parents' house that Friday so I told her we should go see a movie and go out to eat. There was even a movie showing that we had both wanted to see. All she said to my date request was, "We'll see."

We'll see? That was the first time I ever heard that from her. It was always "absolutely" or "sure" if she wanted to go, or "not tonight" if she didn't want to. "We'll see," was just part of her normal vocabulary. Waiting for her to come home that Friday night was kind of like waiting for the grand jury to decide its verdict. Something was going to be decided, and there was a feeling it might not be good for the defendant of the relationship who felt so out of place and couldn't believe he had just heard her say "we'll see."

> **HeaRT #34**: The most subtle changes are easily noticeable, if something's wrong, it will be known

Friday slowly but surely came around and as soon as I got off work for the day I called her up to see about the dinner and a movie. Again, I got the same response. "We'll see." This time it was followed by, "Just come out to my house and we'll talk." When I made my way out to her house she was standing right outside the door even before I got there. Again, this was unusual as she always had waited for me inside whenever I came out to her house. And it was also unusual because the big smile she usually wore was half-hearted. I acted like nothing was wrong and asked, "So how about that movie?" I tried to ask her in a way that sounded like I was excited to go. But she just took a long pause, and said, "We should probably just talk for a little bit first."

"Chris, there's something I really need to tell you."

NO... NOT AGAIN. These were the words that never fail to pierce my heart. "There's something I really need to tell you," always meant either great news or horrific news, and the last week had been leading up to anything but great news. Just like that night when she changed my life from her cell phone at the concert, and it took her a moment to get the words out about how she had liked me ever since grade school, this conversation took a moment of its own to finally get started.

"I'm not sure where to start," she said. A look of worry and confusion was all over her face, like she didn't know how to tell me what she had to say. "I need to explain why everything might've felt so out of place this last week." Being glued to every word she was about to say, I just kept listening. "You know how we always said relationships only work when both people give each other everything they can?"

I said, "Yeah...."

"Well, I just wanted to tell you how much I appreciate it that you have always given me everything you can." She paused for a little bit and then grudgingly forced out her next words as she was beginning to cry, "I just don't think I can give you 100% right now." As soon as she said it she broke out in tears. I was too stunned to react. At first it was hard to understand while she had tears coming out, but she was so sad to have to put an end to something so great, and it must've hurt for her to be the one to end it. A long silent pause went by and I stumbled over my words as I was trying to ask why.

She said, "I just can't, I don't know why, I didn't want it to happen like this, you've always been so good to me." By now she was almost sobbing. It seemed so backwards, she was breaking up with me, but she was the one crying. I was too shocked at the moment to let my emotions do anything at all.

As my brain finally processed the words she was saying, the tears started coming out on my end too. It took so long for me to react that I think my brain was actually trying to reject all of the signals that were being sent to it. My own body was having some type of allergic reaction to what she was saying and my body was naturally trying to reject it.

So he we are, both crying, both knowing something so incredibly fantastic was coming to an end. She was the girl of my dreams, and this was her first real relationship, and it had all gone so incredibly perfect. Neither one of us did anything wrong or made a drastic mistake to be in the situation. As I finally got control of myself I asked what led up to her decision.

"I just need to be single for awhile to figure everything out. I need to move on and try new things while I'm still young enough to do it." Come to find out she had gotten scared that things were getting to the point where the next step in our relationship more than likely involved an engagement ring and that simply scared her to death. She just wasn't ready to make that type of commitment. I wasn't to that point either. It would scare me a little bit too if thoughts and plans of marriage were stuck in my head. "I was never expecting you to commit to anything Steph. You know we always just go with the flow and live day by day." She agreed with me, but still felt that this was the one time in her life where she would be able to take a chance on being single, just to discover what else might be there for her.

Everything just kind of hit me... No more funny faces, no more late night story telling, no more laughing till it hurts, no more lounging in the sun, no more movies, no more kisses from the passenger seat, no more watching television together, no more long trips to see her, no more long kisses good night, no more perky cheeks, no more smoove legs, no more bobble-head doll waves, no more chipmunk smiles, no more I love you's... no more future.

HeaRT #35: Put yourself in their shoes and you will understand the situation much better

It felt like my heart had just been cut out of my chest with a rusty steak knife, then dropped on the ground, and ran over by an army of steamrollers. Although what she was saying hurt so incredibly bad, in an odd way I was admiring what she was doing, proud of someone who was stomping all over my heart. That may sound weird, but as soon as she mentioned, "this is the one chance," I completely understood. *Your heart is free, have the courage to follow it.* She was taking my own advice. *Carpe Diem, Memento Mori!* This probably *was* the one chance for her, being a junior in college, to step out and take a chance that involves being single.

You know you truly and absolutely love someone when you can do nothing but agree with them, love them more, and sit back and watch them rip your heart out. Just like all of our other conversations, this one lasted quite awhile. We kept saying to each other how amazing the relationship was, how fun the ride was, how glad we were to see it all happen, even though now we were both in tears as it was coming to an end. We were both sitting there, wiping the tears out of our eyes, and I stopped and said to her in a half-crackled voice from crying, "good thing we pinky swore, huh."

> **HeaRT #36**: Don't forget your promises

In-between the tears she started to laugh a little bit too. Her mouth showed a grin, but the rest of her face was still crying. As she was smiling through her sobbing, she says, "I was thinking the exact same thing. How is it we always know what the other one is thinking?" We both started to laugh a little more than we were crying. Not the typical break up scene, we were truly just two friends, bound by a pinky swear, sitting there talking. And now we were laughing. Somehow we *always* found a way to laugh with each other.

We were outside the whole time, just standing in her yard, looking each other squarely in the eye, talking to each other and watching one another let out the tears. She wanted it to work, but at the same time she had to follow her heart and take a chance, there was no other way, that's just how we are. Then she said, "Time just kind of ran out." At the time, I didn't want to believe those words, and even now I don't fully understand how time could "run out." My clock was still ticking, my time was eternity. I'm always going to love her, but now I had to let her go.

My Proof

"To love is to receive a glimpse of heaven."
- Karen Sunde

Maybe it had something to do with the rush of emotions, maybe it had something to do with the autumn sunset, maybe it had something to do with the breeze blowing through her hair, and maybe it was just the look in her eyes, but during that conversation, I realized I was having to let go of a true to life, heaven-sent blessing.

"Steph, do you realize that things like this just don't happen everyday? Things like this don't even happen in most people's lifetime. What are the odds that we would both be in love with each other for so long without saying anything, and then after a decade, finally come together? The last two years we have shared some of the most incredible times that we will both never forget. This kind of stuff just doesn't happen for no reason you know." As I was saying all of this, I was realizing there was one very important reason it all happened. To me, Steph really was heaven-sent. That evening I realized that all along, ever since the first grade, I have had a crush on an angel, and she *had* to know what she meant to me.

> **HeaRT #37**: Make sure you mean it when you tell someone how incredibly special they are

"Steph, there's something I really need to tell you."

Finally... I was the one who got to say the words, *there's something I really need to tell you.* "I hope you're not mad at me for saying this, but to tell the truth, before I started dating you, I've never really truly believed in everything I hear at church. My whole life I have always needed a reason for why things are the way they are. For some reason, if I don't know the way things work, if I don't have proof, I don't believe in them. No matter what someone has ever told me, I never believed them until they showed me proof. I don't mean to scare you, but I'm not sure I really ever believed in any type of religion because I've never had proof." By that time, she had a really confused look on her face. Why would I be talking about this stuff now?

"But I just wanted to tell you, that you are my proof. You're that one thing that gives me a reason to believe that there is something good in this world, something worth believing in, and something worth living for. You're my angel Steph."

As I was talking, her eyes got real big and her jaw dropped to the ground. I was just telling her what I was feeling and telling her exactly how I honestly felt. She was astonished what I was saying and just froze with the look on her face that was saying, "No one has ever said anything like this to me." I looked into her eyes and said, "But I mean it Steph, you really are my proof." I glanced up at the sky and told her, "You really are what makes me believe there's something up there looking down on us."

No matter where I go, I always carry around a picture of me and Steph. If anyone ever challenges my belief on the existence of a heaven, all I have to do is pull out the picture, point at her and say, "This is Steph, she's an angel from heaven, and I personally know her." That is why I know there is a heaven.

Our conversation eventually came to an end. Believe it or not, there was nothing left to say. She had made it clear of what she wanted, and ironically I was proud of her for what she was doing. If it had been any one of our normal conversations, by this time I would have said "I got nothing." This time, I didn't have to say it, the feeling was already there. *I got nothing.* The one thing that mattered most in my life no longer loved me like she used to. I really did have nothing. When we were both done talking all we could do was look at each other, and try not to cry.

She gave me a big hug when I was leaving, and all she could say was, "I'm so, so sorry." She couldn't completely stop herself from crying and I couldn't hold it back either. To try to cheer us both up I said, "Hey, don't ever forget about the pinky swear." I reached out with my pinky, and once more we promised by the shake of the smallest finger on our right hands that we would always be friends, no matter what.

> **HeaRT #38**: Make your goodbyes count

Now What?

For the most part, I held up fairly well during our conversation. The crying was kept under control enough to listen and talk, but on the drive home I was bawling my eyes out. Yes, there are men on this earth who aren't afraid to admit they not only cry, but they bawl. I just didn't know what to do or how to react. I just let the emotions carry me away. When I made it home, I took a deep breath and told myself that I would just have to face the facts and do whatever I had to do to keep living. At that point it hurt so bad that sheer survival seemed it was at risk. How could I live? How could life ever be any better? Nothing else ever mattered more than Steph, now what do I do?

Even though my date plans of a dinner and a movie had been totally wiped off the map that night, I still had something to do without her. My uncle was having his retirement party that night and most of my family was going to be there. After I sat at home for awhile in shock, I took a mildly refreshing shower and made my way out to the party hoping none of my family or friends would notice that I had spent the last few hours in tears. Luckily it was dark enough by then that no one could notice my weepy eyes.

While I was at the retirement party, my cell phone rang and it was my brother-in-law on the phone. "Hey, do you want to come to a basketball game with me?" Part of me wanted to say, "No, I'd rather go home, crawl in a hole, and die." Luckily, the other part of me was saying, "Just go and get your mind on something else." Growing up I thought there was nothing more important than basketball. Now I had come full circle. After going through absolute love, basketball meant nearly nothing to me. It took almost seven years for me to realize it, but Coach Quinn (my high school basketball coach) was right. There *are* more important things in life than basketball. How fitting that the most important thing in my life at the time was what made me realize it. All I could think about was Steph. After the game, on the way back to the parking lot, without even thinking, I dialed her number. There was not a single hesitation in calling her as it had become an involuntary routine by then. As the phone was ringing I had to stop and remind myself that the best thing to happen in my life wasn't happening anymore. She's no longer mine.

She was so nice to actually answer the phone and talk to me just like always. But of course it wasn't the same. Most girls in that situation would probably just shut their phones off and hang me out to dry. But not Steph, she always had the decency and respect not to ignore someone. It was only a few hours since she dropped the heart-hammer, and she was still continuing to do things that made me love her even more.

I can't thank her enough for being nice enough to talk on the phone to me rather than ignoring my call. It helped so much just to be able to hear her voice. She didn't even have to say anything that made sense, all I needed to hear was her voice. The same being that had turned my life upside down, was the only person I wanted to turn to in order to ease the pain. It was an odd combination. She broke my heart, but at the same time was the first person I wanted to talk to in order to begin the emotional therapy.

> **HeaRT #39**: Doing the little things for someone with a broken heart help tremendously

Immobilized

"When you have a heart the size of Texas, it really hurts when it breaks."

- Chris Miller

When I was getting out of my bed the next morning, I actually had to stop and think twice whether or not everything had just happened the night before. I even had to stop and make sure our entire relationship had actually happened. Was it all just a dream? It sure was possible that I had been sleeping the whole time and somehow I had some sort of dream that allows you to vividly and specifically experience very particular and incredibly beautiful things in your sleep. Maybe none of it had happened at all. As I was crawling out of my bed, wondering if it really had happened, I looked on the floor and saw my t-shirt which was worn the night before. It was still wrinkled and a little bit damp towards the bottom where I had used it to wipe the tears from my eyes when I was talking to Steph. It must have been real, because I had proof. I had proof that I had lost my ultimate proof. Steph was real, I was real, and our relationship was real. The biggest dream of my life *had* come true...

But now it was over.

That morning, getting out of bed was difficult. What did I need to get out of bed for? There was no reason to wake up knowing I might never get to go on another date with Steph and that I might never get another kiss from her again. Not a single thing the rest of my life would ever mean anything more to me than our relationship.

Nothing would mean more, but I was scheduled to work that morning. At the time I was a part time teller at the bank in my hometown. That morning I walked into the bank trying to act as if nothing had happened the night before. Maybe working would actually keep my mind off of my broken heart. Working as a teller at a bank isn't the most physically demanding job in the world. Actually it is very easy and there isn't much that would physically stop someone from being able to do the job.

> **HeaRT #40**: The worst thing to do with a broken heart is to sit still

On Saturday mornings it was always just two tellers who worked, and this morning it was Irma and me. Irma is a veteran teller at the bank and one of the nicest ladies in the world. When I walked in the door, I said hi to Irma and tried to act normal. Usually we were fairly talkative for Saturday mornings, but this time I just said "good morning" and nothing else. After only a few minutes of being at work, my thoughts fixated on the night before. I tried to resist it, but my body wanted to cry more than it wanted to work. Eventually I had to stop, blow my nose, wipe away a few tears and said, "Irma, I think I need to go home. I just can't work right now." There was no explanation as to why I couldn't, plus I didn't want to talk about it. Being a wise old woman, Irma more than likely caught the drift of what was going on. She just said, "That's fine, you'll feel better tomorrow." It was almost as if she could just sense what I was going through.

The entire day all I could think about was, "What went wrong? What led up to her decision? Why did it have to end? How was it that she loved me in the first place? How did one girl have the power to change my life so much? Why couldn't I work? Why does it hurt so badly? Was there any way I could have stopped it from ending? Was there something I failed to do? Is there something I can do about it?"

That night I couldn't sleep at all. I was still asking myself a million questions and eventually became obsessed with the last one, "Is there something I can do about it?"

Although I had understood and respected why she made her decision in the first place, something inside wasn't going to let it go without one last hoorah. After thinking about it for awhile, I came up with the perfect solution.

> **HeaRT #41**: Never leave the possibility for regrets, Always ask yourself, "What have I got to lose?"

She's Lost That Loving Feeling

One of Steph's favorite movies is Top Gun. There's a scene where Maverick (played by Tom Cruise) serenades Charlie (played by Kelly McGillis) with a song by the Righteous Brothers. This would be the perfect way to show her what she means to me. It would be just the thing! All I need is a pair of big shiny sunglasses and a CD with the song and I'm set. There was one small problem. I didn't have any big, silver-rimmed sunglasses. I couldn't sleep and I couldn't bear to wait to make sure I had everything in place. So at three in the morning I found myself driving to Wal-Mart to get a pair of goofy sunglasses and was listening to a CD I had just made on my computer with the song I was about to sing the next day. I just needed to double check to make sure I knew all the words.

The next day I drove out to Steph's house and walked into the living room where she was sitting on the couch. I walked in with a big grin on my face and told her that there was something I needed to show her. I'm not sure if I was grinning because I was about to make an absolute fool of myself or because I thought there was a chance I was about to change her mind. At any rate, I grabbed the TV remote (my makeshift microphone) that was lying on the coffee table, got on one knee, tried to hide my grin, and started singing my song:

> *You never close your eyes anymore*
> *When I kiss your lips*
> *And there's no tenderness like before*
> *In your fingertips*
> *You're trying hard not to show it*
> *But baby, baby I know it*
>
> *You've lost that loving feeling*
> *Oh, that loving feeling*
> *You've lost that loving feeling*
> *Now it's gone, gone, gone*
> *Whoa-oh...*

She just smiled through the whole song. No one in the room, including myself, could believe I was actually doing this. I'm a horrible singer to start with, but the performance actually wasn't that bad. After I sang my song, I gave her a list of my top 10 reasons why she should stay with me and follow through…

10. I will miss those perky cheeks.

9. I'd give anything up for you.
   • The Past (I took a chance by letting go of a past relationship. It was worth it.)
   • Time (I quit my job so I could spend more time with you. It was worth it.)
   • Money (I'd buy anything for you just to make you smile: a purse from the GAP, a diamond necklace from Greenbergs, or just enough gas for my car to surprise you on a Thursday night.) It was all worth it.

8. I am willing to completely embarrass myself in front of anyone and everyone just to show you how much I love you.

7. We understand each other better than we understand or own selves sometimes.

6. I would never do anything to hurt you, and you've known me since you can remember.

5. Our first kiss was unbelievable, I doubt it's possible to have a better first kiss.

4. When we're together, we forget about everything and are absolute goofballs who always find a way to make each other laugh.

3. I've dreamed about being with you ever since I knew you. I've liked you since the first grade (What other guys are you going to meet that can

say that?) Even in high school we still had crushes on each other. You went your way and I went mine... but eventually we found each other and once we were together, I had the time of my life, and I could tell you did too.

2. You're my proof, my reason to believe that there's something good in this world.

1. If you stay by my side, I can promise you and I can guarantee, I will be there for you, and I will love you like no one else can... for as long as I live.

My best effort was given to do everything I could to show her just how much she means to me and to show her she was letting go of someone who loved her more than anything in the world. But she didn't budge. There was no response. She was rock solid on her decision. Her mind had been made up long before I had the chance to do anything about it, and there really wasn't anything I could have done anyways. No matter what, I always made sure to treat her right and she always got the best from me. But it was all over now. I had to let it go. She just didn't want to be committed and there was nothing I could do about it.

> **HeaRT #42**: All the reasons in the world won't mean much; it's what *they* feel on the inside that matters

Chapter 6

My Last E-mail

Exactly three weeks after she broke up with me I sent her an email. This time I wasn't trying to change her mind. I just needed to tell her thanks.

```
Steph,

I was debating writing all of this down
or calling you up and talking to you on
the phone about it, but I guess I'll
start by writing it down.

Sorry if it's a long email, but there's a
lot I want to say to you, and maybe now is
the wrong time to say it all, but I just
can't help but think, what if tomorrow
never comes and something happens where I
wish I would have told you everything.  I
just want you to know too that I'm not
saying this stuff to try to change your
mind.  You want to be single for awhile
and I respect that, but I just wanted to
say how I feel so I won't have to wonder
in the future if things would have turned
out differently if you would have known
exactly how I feel about you.
```

Help a Kid in Love

If now is the wrong time, if you've got other things in your life to think about and to figure out, please just stop right here and read this some other day.

I'm not sure if I really need to say all of this, and maybe you don't feel the same way about it as me, but I figured I'd just say it so here goes...

When we first started dating, we agreed that we both needed to wait three weeks to make sure that what we were doing was right and both thought that three weeks would be enough time to let everything clear up.

Well, it's been three weeks since that day you told me you need to be single and I guess I feel like I'm finally understanding the situation and also understand what I'm really feeling right now and there's some things I need to say just to get them off my chest.

First of all I just wanted to tell you thanks. Thanks for being who you are, thanks for sharing your time with me, thanks for giving me a chance, thanks for helping me become a better person, and most of all, thanks for making my wildest dream come true.

You have had such a huge impact on my life as you have made me such a better person now than I was a year and a half ago. I'm a better person in so many ways, and it's all because of you. The way I see life, my attitude, my faith, the fun I have, how I value my friends and family, and the way I communicate with people is all better because of you. Maybe most people will look at me and see the same person they've always known me as and I'm sure on the outside there aren't many changes, but if you or anyone else could be me for a minute or two, they could understand all of the things on the inside that were changed for the better just from being with you. I mean it from the bottom of my heart when I say thanks. Maybe you never thought that you would have such a dramatic influence on someone's life, but the love you gave me completely changed my life for the better and I can't thank you enough.

I also wanted to thank you for giving me the best memories of my life. There are times we shared and things we've done that felt so incredible and were better than all the best dreams I've ever had. I will never forget the times I spent with you. From all the small times I tried to show you that I liked you while we were in high school, to that night we talked for hours at the graduation party, to that night you called me on the phone from the concert, to our first kiss (and all the good ones after that), for the times we said I love you, for all the times I came up to your dorm just to be a bum, all the times we swam in your pool and sat out and tanned, all the tennis matches, all the movies we saw together, all the dates we went on, and most importantly the millions of times we just sat and laughed with each other....

It's too bad we didn't keep track, but I seriously wonder how many times we laughed together. I remember that one day when your sister asked if that's all we do is laugh, and I remember your roommate making a similar comment. But that's what I miss the most right now is just laughing with you.

When I look back at all the time I spent with you, to me it all seems like a crazy kind of blur. It was so unbelievable that it feels like it was all just a dream, but at the same time it felt so real. I've never felt anything like it, but I know for sure that it was knock-you-down, make your knees week, out of this world, bottom of the 9th grand slam, complete, real, true, pure, absolute love.

I never thought that I would ever be so much in love, have so much fun, and mostly be that lucky. When I woke up that Saturday morning after you told me you need to be single, I actually had to stop and think if the last year and a half was really just a dream. Everything just seemed so perfect. If I go to Heaven, that's what I want it to be like... I would give up everything I have right now, if I could spend the rest of my days feeling like I did when I was with you.

You're right when you say who knows what will happen next. Maybe there's something better that will come along in both of our lives and we'll both be happier than we ever were, or maybe we'll find each other again somehow. All I know is that so far I have had a wonderful life and I've been blessed with so many things that I shouldn't take for granted. I just wanted to let you know that you are at the top of my list of all the great things I've had in my life. I knew it before, I knew it when I was with you, and I know now that you are something special. It's so hard for me to let you be on your own and leave everything to chance.

But it's getting better, I've finally come to the point where I'm alright with you wanting to be on your own. What's really ironic is that the way you're handling the situation is exactly how I would try if I was in your shoes and I'm so glad that you're doing everything you can to make it easier on me, and also making it work that we will still be friends.

I understand why you're making this decision especially at this time in your life. You're right that this is probably the one chance for you to be single and probably the last time you will actually want to be single and free and I'm sure you're going to have a blast and hopefully you can look back on your life with no regrets.

You're also absolutely right when you say you're either with someone, or you're not. If two people can't give 100% to each other than there's no reason for the relationship to go on. If it does, someone eventually gets hurt down the road way worse than if someone would have had the guts to say what needed to be said. What you had to do is one of the hardest things in life, trust me I know. It's so hard to have to say something to someone when you know it is going to break their heart. Thank you for coming out and saying what needed to be said, because it took a lot of courage and it needed to be done if you were feeling what you were feeling.

So I just wanted to tell you thanks for being a bigger person, being honest, and doing what you had to do. Now that I sit back and look at it, I'm glad you broke up with me when you did because you did it before things went downhill and all I have right now are perfect memories of you and me that weren't ruined by trying to force things to happen and drag it along by trying to make things work when you knew that you really just needed to be single right now.

The other thing I wanted to say thanks for was being the girl of my dreams (literally) in every way imaginable. Even now, I feel like there was absolutely nothing missing about you. There's nothing I would change if I could, and there is nothing else I would rather have. I've never felt that way about any other person in my life. Some people say that in order to truly love someone you have to see through their faults. From day one I didn't see the slightest hint to any faults and there was nothing I had to see through or try not to think about. It was all perfect and all natural.

Your personality, your smile, your cheeks, your laugh, your voice, your sense of humor, your family, where you come from, your friends, your hair, your smoove legs, your cute clothes, your amazing body, your athletic abilities, the random things you say and do that make me laugh, your short little toes, the way you kiss, your loving and carefree attitude, your thoughts, your actions, your way of looking at life.... I could make a list a mile long. Everything was perfect.

Not only was everything perfect about you, I thought everything was perfect about us as a couple too.

It had it all.

Trust, friendship, attraction, patience, amazing kisses, no arguments, no problem with forgiveness, the laughter, the ability to make each other happy when the other was sad, always being able to talk, always being able to understand, never taking each other for granted, treating each other right, respecting each other, just being nice, just having fun, just living day by day, going with the flow, thinking about things the same way, finishing my sentences, always being able to guess what I had to tell you, and always happy to see each other.... I can't think of anything that I would change about the way we were.

I just can't believe how it was possible that things could be so perfect, both with you as an individual and us as a couple. It just feels so amazing. Sometimes things are too good to be true... but with us, for me anyways, things were as good as it gets, and as true as it could be, and they're wasn't anything unreal about it.

Maybe this isn't a mutual feeling, and maybe you feel differently, or maybe you're not sure what to think about it at all. What I do know is that it had to be real love for you too. I know you wanted it to work just as bad as I did, I know you had as much fun as I did, and I know you would never hurt somebody if you didn't have to.

I just hope that I gave you everything you wanted out of your first real relationship. I'm kind of glad that I got to be the first too, because I always wanted to be with you, and I just wanted to show you what love can do. I'm always afraid that you might run into some other guy that doesn't give you everything you deserve.

I know it's only been three weeks, but I can tell that there is no way that I'm ever going to be able to be completely over you. Everything went way too well and it was everything I ever wanted. This is my way of telling you that as long as we're both single, I can guarantee you that if you want to come back to me, consider yourself mine in a heartbeat. We would be happy forever no matter what happened or where we went.

Someday I may find a way to move on, but it is going to take someone just as unbelievable as you to make it happen. I never got a chance to tell you, but there is not a single aspect of my life where I want to be "content."

There are so many big dreams I want to come true, and when I set goals, they are sky high. All I know is that I'm not going to have any regrets with my life and I'm not going to look back and have to say someday, "I wonder what would have happened if I would've tried this or that." I'm not afraid of failing in life. I'm afraid of not living life and trying to get exactly what I want.

What I exactly want to do in life is to travel the world and see everything that I can, while helping as many people as possible. I love going places, seeing things, and learning something new. I want to accomplish as much as I can in one lifetime and want to see all my wildest dreams come true. Of all my big crazy dreams, you were always the biggest.

Help a Kid in Love

I've always had these big dreams in my head, but thanks to you, now I actually have the courage to pursue them. Maybe some of my big crazy dreams won't come true, but at least I will know for sure that I did all I could to find out. Thanks for teaching me to be the guy to speak up and that if you're going to dream, why not dream big.

I just want you to know that you've always been my biggest, craziest dream. I never, ever thought that I'd get to be with you, but the awesome thing is, even though I don't know what will happen now, is that I know one of my craziest dreams has came true because you gave me a chance. All I wanted was to just be with you. I didn't need to be married to you, or live forever with you. All I needed was one kiss, and one chance to be in love with you. And I got that kiss and that chance, and now that one of my biggest dreams came true, I don't see why any of my other big crazy dreams can't materialize. This is one of those ways that you've changed my life. I've always had big dreams, but you were the first one that actually came true for me, and now I'm looking at life completely differently. Thank you so much for showing me that my dreams really can come true.

When I decided to take a chance on you, I had no idea everything would go so well. In the back of my head I was kind of thinking that maybe I would find out that I was just obsessed with wanting to be with you and that it might just be a letdown once I was actually with you. But there was only one way to find out, and what I did find, is that you are the best thing in the world for me, and are everything I've ever wanted and dreamed of, and then some! All I needed to tell was that first kiss. Maybe you should kiss some other guys so you have something to compare to, but I'm not lying when I say that there was something magical about that night and I still can't believe it was so perfect.

I'm not one that believes in destiny, I think we are responsible for making the choices that God puts in front of us. I have this feeling that no matter how things end up, we are both going to be happy whether we're together or not because we both just live life and make it how we want it to be with no regrets.

So now I'm just trying to move on with my life and roll with the punches, but I don't want you to think at all that I'm giving up on you. I think that you still love me on the inside, but you know that you have to be on your own for now.

Don't think for a second that I'm going to stop loving you, but at the same time I don't want you to think that I'm putting everything off for you, and that I'm just going to sit by my phone waiting for you to call. I would like to move on with my life and see what's in store for me.

There's a chance I might find something different that is right for me, but all I know is that I found everything I wanted with you and it's literally impossible for me to find another girl that I've liked for so long.

So I think I just wrote everything that's been running around in my head right now. I'm sorry I had to write a novel, and like I said I'm not at all trying to change your mind because I just really needed to get all of this off my chest. So thanks so much if you've read all of this. I'm not expecting you to write anything back or call me back. I just wanted to get everything out and tell you how I feel.

All of this comes from the bottom of my heart and I mean it. I have seriously been bawling my eyes out writing most of this, and I'm not the type of person to cry either.

But mostly I just wanted to say

Thanks for Everything Steph,

Chris Miller

I Love you More than Anything,
and I'll Love You until the day I die.

Main Entry: ¹**love**
Pronunciation: ' l ɛv
Function: *noun*
Etymology: Middle English, from Old English *lufu;* akin to Old High German *luba* love, Old English *lEof* dear, Latin *lubEre, libEre* to please

1 a (1) : strong affection for another arising out of kinship or personal ties <maternal *love* for a child> (2) : attraction based on sexual desire : affection and tenderness felt by lovers (3) : affection based on admiration, benevolence, or common interests <*love* for his old schoolmates> **b** : an assurance of love <give her my *love*>

2 : warm attachment, enthusiasm, or devotion <*love* of the sea>

3 a : the object of attachment, devotion, or admiration <baseball was his first *love*> **b** (1) : a beloved person : **DARLING** -- often used as a term of endearment (2) *British* -- used as an informal term of address

4 a : unselfish loyal and benevolent concern for the good of another: as (1) : the fatherly concern of God for humankind (2) : brotherly concern for others **b** : a person's adoration of God

5 : a god or personification of love

6 : an amorous episode : **LOVE AFFAIR**

7 : the sexual embrace : **COPULATION**

8 : a score of zero (as in tennis)

9 *capitalized, Christian Science* : **GOD**

- **at love** : holding one's opponent scoreless in tennis
- **in love** : inspired by affection

Main Entry: ²love
Function: *verb*
Inflected Form(s): **loved; loving**
transitive verb
1 : to hold dear : CHERISH
2 a : to feel a lover's passion, devotion, or tenderness for b (1) : CARESS (2) : to fondle amorously (3) : to copulate with
3 : to like or desire actively : take pleasure in <*loved* to play the violin>
4 : to thrive in <the rose *loves* sunlight>
intransitive verb : to feel affection or experience desire

(Dictionary entries can be viewed online at www.m-w.com)

Help a Kid in Love

Chapter 7

The Power and Endurance of Absolute Love

Words are wonderful. With the use of words you can explain and express all of the invisible intangibles in the world. Sometimes it's hard to find the right words to express yourself and sometimes it hard to fully understand a word. But it is amazing how big of an impact four letters, one word, and one feeling can have. It's also amazing how difficult it is to define love with other words. The best-selling book of all time, the Bible, uses 81 words to describe absolute love.

1 Corinthians 13 : 4-7, 13

Love is patient, love is kind. It is not jealous, is not pompous, it is not inflated, it is not rude, it does not seek its own interests, it is not quick-tempered, it does not brood over injury, it does not rejoice over wrongdoing but rejoices with the truth. It bears all things, believes all things, hopes all things, endures all things. Love never fails.

Three things will always remain—faith, hope, and love—and the greatest of these is love.

Even Noah Webster has a hard time defining love. Type in "love" on his online dictionary and you're given 12 different definitions of love (13 if you count *a score of zero, as in tenni*s.) It's so confusing that it's a noun and a verb.

While I was looking up Webster's definition of love I also checked to see what he had to say about the word absolute. He says absolute means free from imperfection, standing apart from, having no restriction, exception, or qualification. Absolute is positive, unquestionable, ultimate, and perfectly embodies the nature of a thing.

By combining the words absolute and love, you arrive at the apex of exactly how I feel about Steph. To me she was free from imperfection, (refer back to my email for proof.) She easily stood apart from everything else in my life. We always had so much fun together as we were free from restrictions, exceptions and qualifications. Without a doubt, my feelings for her are the ultimate embodiment of the nature of love.

I never heard the term absolute love before I wrote the first draft of this book, but as I started researching a little bit, I discovered there were other people who used the term absolute love to explain feelings of love that do incredible things and have a very profound impact on their life. One description I found compared absolute love to a fire.

> *"The power of absolute love*
> *is a raging fire of uncontainable majesty*
> *that consumes any and all*
> *who come too close to its flames."*
>
> - Andrew Cohen

By Mr. Cohen's definition of absolute love, I guess you could say I got burned. I came too close to its flames and was consumed. Originally I was thinking of something other than a fire for my personal description of absolute love; however, it has the same connotations.

Above All

Absolute love is above all
Highest on anyone's subconscious priority list,
It transcends everything,
walks through walls, never gives up,
patiently waits, doesn't ask questions,
and never takes a day off
Absolute love spans across countries
and does not recognize time
It trumps age, hatred, and violence
Knows no limits and has no boundaries
There's no chance to turn it down or ignore it
It cannot be contained
It cannot be quieted
It is inescapable
It's an unavoidable walk across a bed of nails
to serve up your heart on a silver platter
while not demanding, expecting,
or even wishing for a single thing in return

Help a Kid in Love

Although I can only offer my opinion, it is my belief that absolute love is not only the most important thing in the world, but also the most powerful. Napoleon Hill might describe it as a mystical force floating around in the air for anyone to use. It's a force that made me write a book, start a website, and step outside my comfort zone. It's what makes me want to help everyone in the world find a way past their broken heart, and has allowed me to learn and accomplish things faster than I ever have before. It's my fuel that allows me to go places, meet people, and do incredible things. It's what's going to allow me to tell the *entire* world that I love Steph.

Absolute love is also what has set me free. The word absolute comes from the Latin word *absolutus,* from past participle of *absolvere,* to set free. On the surface, when you hear the word absolute, static thoughts of permanency and certainty come to mind. But when you dig deeper, and get to the core of the word absolute, you find it's an explosive force that offers freedom which opens countless doors to limitless opportunities.

Before being with Steph, my attitude towards life was much more passive than now. Forever stuck in my mind is the day she told me that all I had to do was ask her out and she probably would have said yes. While I was always agonizing over the thought of rejection, she was always waiting for me to ask. That's all I needed to do. Because it was absolute love, now I know that if you are sure of something, if there's something you desire more than anything, if there's something you've always wanted in your life, it just might want to be with you too. All you have to do is ask. Steph was just as attracted to me all those years through school as I was to her.

But I never asked. Once you experience absolute love, the fear of rejection vanishes.

What do you want out of life? Have you asked for it yet?

I Bargained with Life for a Penny…

I bargained with Life for a penny,
And Life would pay no more,
However I begged at evening,
When I counted my scanty store.
For Life is a just employer,
He gives you what you ask,
But once you have set the wages,
Why, you must bear the task.
I worked for a menial's hire,
Only to learn, dismayed,
That any wage I had asked of Life,
Life would have willingly paid.

- Jessie Belle Rittenhouse (1869–1948)

It took 13 years since being in love with that cute blond hair girl in first grade to finally learn that she would have always said yes. After going through our relationship, after waiting so long, it was a slap in the face to learn that all I had to do was ask. Absolute love has been my greatest teacher of taking action and forgetting about failure.

Love in its absoluteness is what wrote this book. It used the body and mind of a 21 year old to organize its thoughts and feelings into words, paragraphs, and chapters.

Help a Kid in Love

Without absolute love this book would never had existed and you would not be holding it in your hand. The thoughts may have still been in my head, but because Steph was her, and I loved her so, this book has become a reality. Again, absolute love is inescapable, unavoidable, and undeniable. You can't get rid of it and you can't hide it. The most logical and productive thing to do about absolute love is to recognize it and use it. Harnessing the power and using it to your benefit will be explained in further detail in the next chapter.

All of the Above

It was interesting to learn so much about love while writing this book. Originally, I had the impression that love was this universal thing that was relatively the same for every person in every place in time. However, I learned this is not the case. Granted, it is simply when you care for someone (thanks again Abby!) but the how and why of caring for them can vary widely as you move from one type of love to the other. When this book was published, the world's largest encyclopedia recognized ten different types of love.

(From Wikipedia.com)

- ✓ Courtly love – a late medieval conventionalized code prescribing certain conduct and emotions for ladies and their lovers
- ✓ Erotic love – affection characterized by sexual desires
- ✓ Familial love – affection brokered through kinship connections, intertwined with concepts of attachment and bonding
- ✓ Free love – loving relations according to choice and unrestricted by marriage
- ✓ Platonic love – a close relationship in which sexual desire is non-existent or has been suppressed or sublimated
- ✓ Puppy love – romantic affection that is not "mature" or not "true." The term is often used with negative connotations, insinuating that love between youngsters is less genuine or valuable
- ✓ Religious love – devotion to one's deity or theology
- ✓ Romantic love – affection characterized by a mix of emotional intimacy and sexual desire
- ✓ True love – love without condition, motive or attachment. Loving someone just because they are themselves, not their actions or beliefs in particular
- ✓ Unrequited love – affection and desire not reciprocated or returned

It was very interesting to discover all the specific kinds of love. As I went through the list I read each description and made a mental note in my mind about what each type of love might look like in the real world. After I finished reading through the entire list, I went back to the top, and in a checklist fashion marked the types of love I was able to experience because of Steph. What was really odd was that by the time I got to the bottom of the list I realized that in some way, shape, or form I had experienced every single type of love over the course of being in love with Steph for the past 15 years, which makes up two-thirds of my entire life.

Courtly love – Steph conventionalized the code of waiting three weeks before we did anything irrational.

Erotic love – There was always a natural, primal attraction.

Familial love – Our families were very close friends. Also we were 2 of 11 classmates that sat in the same classroom together from the first day of kindergarten all the way until graduation. I consider this group of classmates my family and I most certainly care for all of them; therefore it is love.

Free love – Steph freely chose to be with me, I freely chose to be with her, and we never were bound by marriage.

Platonic love – We both valued waiting until marriage before going all the way.

Puppy love – I disagree with the connotations that young love is less genuine or valuable. My 4 year old sister is proof that age is not a requirement to understand love. However, you could call the feelings I had for Steph in the first grade puppy love as they were not yet completely "mature."

Religious love – Thanks to Steph, my proof, I am capable of believing in higher power.

True love – Although I listed many particular details throughout the book about why I specifically love Steph, in the end I love her just because she is always herself, always genuine. I may appear heavily attached, but in the next chapter you will discover I'm actually the opposite of attached.

Unrequited love – Do I even need to explain this one?

Out of the ten types listed, unrequited love is by far the most life changing love of all. It was the most interesting to read in further detail and anyone looking to capitalize on a broken heart must become a student of unrequited love if they wish to catapult forward with my philosophy.

As I finished going through each type of love, it was really odd that I could relate every single one of them to Steph. Some types applied tighter than others, but nonetheless all were valid associations. Is there anyone in your life who played a part in your of all ten types? Try to go through this list with the ones you love. If you can make an association with each and every type of love listed, than you know exactly how I feel. After going through this list I realized they had left out the most important type of love of all. I believe they need to add one more type of love right underneath unrequited love.

My Addition: **Absolute Love**

My Definition: **All of the Above**

I mentioned earlier that absolute love is "above all," and in great irony here it is appearing to be "all of the above." How's that for genius of AND, Mr. Collins! Absolute love is above all AND all of the above. You could say it's the alpha *and* the omega, beginning *and* the end, most painful *and* most blissful, permanently committed *and* setting you free. It's so pure, simple, true *and* so incredibly mystifying.

If you would walk across a bed of nails to serve up your heart on a silver platter without demanding, expecting, or even wishing for a single thing in return; if it feels like you have been consumed by the flames of a raging fire of uncontainable majesty; if you can honestly check off the first ten types of love on the list, it is highly likely, almost certain, that the real type of love you feel for this person is absolute.

It might be different than what you may have expected, but you have just experienced the complete embodiment of the nature of love. You now know the power and endurance of *absolute* love. How does it feel? It hurts a little bit doesn't it? But yet, it still feels so incredible, so wonderful, and so powerful! Soak it up, enjoy it, embrace it, and just bask in its bliss, even if there is a dash of pain attached.

Chris Miller

In Every Language, I Love Her

Chinese Character of Love

Loosely translated as:
"a breath of wind that sets you free"

If you love someone as absolutely as I do, wouldn't you like to tell the entire world you love them? It should be clear by now and you should fully understand what is driving me to tell every person in every country on every continent that I love Steph. I love her because I care for her, and it is ABSOLUTE! I'm psyched, I'm pumped, and I'm in love! I'm ready to make history and tell the *entire* world! But wait, I only speak English. The *entire* world doesn't speak English... that's a problem. I need to translate my love into every world language in order to reach my goal.

If you thought it was tough defining exactly what the word love means, just wait until you see what it takes to fully and simply explain love in its totality... in each and every global language. You would think you could just open up a translation book and substitute one word for the other. I have discovered that is not the case. Translating is a tough job. People who speak English take the word love for granted. As hard as it is completely defining it, everyone who speaks English at least has a broad sense of what you're saying when you use the word love.

Now imagine yourself trying to explain the word love to a tribe of African natives, Australian Aborigines, or billions of people in China that use a symbol that looks like a fancy stick person with a funny looking hat on its head that is *loosely* translated into the English language as "a breath of wind that sets you free." It was hard enough explaining just one word in one language, now I have to explain seven words that are talking about the wind and not a feeling between two people.

Writing one book in one language is hard enough, effectively translating your book into every global language makes writing just one book seem like it was an article clipped out of your local newspaper. But love, especially absolute love, always finds a way. As you are reading this, I am hard at work, finding ways to translate this book into every language on the planet. In the last chapter, I provide more information about how you can help me translate Help a Kid in Love into all the global languages so I can help the entire world get through their heartache.

All I Wanted For Christmas

It was in the middle of October when I was 20 years old when she completed the cycle and broke my heart. It took quite some time for me to fully realize that it was absolute love. By that following Christmas, I was still having an incredibly difficult time letting go.

Chris Miller

It's materialistic American tradition to make a long list of things you don't need as Christmas comes near. Every year in the past I joined in on the Christmas spirit and fixated my thoughts on what doo-dads, toys, and clothes I wanted. Hitting rock bottom puts a different spin on the usual holiday cheer. That year I didn't ask for a single thing. I was committing a middle class American sin by not creating a Christmas list that year. It wasn't that I was too lazy to put together a list. I couldn't have made one if I tried. There wasn't anything else that mattered, they're wasn't anything I wanted, at least anything my parents, or even Santa Claus could give me.

My mom was the first one to notice that I was behind on posting a Christmas list. She said to me multiple times during the month of December, "If you don't write anything down, no one's going to know what to buy you." Whenever she said that I'd just silently respond in my head, "You can't buy what I want." So I guess you could say that I did have a list. It was a mental list, a very specific list, and there was one thing I wanted more than anything. Here was my Christmas list for 2005:

<u>Chris's Christmas List</u>

1. Steph

That's it. That's all I want. That's all that matters to me. My birthday is December, 23rd, so you could consider that my birthday wish list as well. And you don't even have to take it off the refrigerator; just leave it up there for next year. And Santa can just keep one copy of my list at the

North Pole. I won't be making a new list next year. It will just be the exact same thing.

> *"Nothing can take the taste of peanut butter out of your mouth like unrequited love."*
>
> - Charlie Brown

A Little Effort, and a Little Heart, Go a Long Way

As you are beginning to see, absolute love really does make you do unexpected and unimaginable things. I would have never thought that someday I would be writing and translating an entire book into every language on the planet. It all started when one girl sat in a desk in the first grade and it has gradually grown ever since. It took quite some time for me to finally realize that it was absolute love. Throughout our entire relationship, Steph never asked of or demanded anything from me. All she ever wanted to do was have fun, relax, and enjoy each day as it came. That was one very important lesson she taught me, and is one of the many reasons that I am incapable of not loving her. Very similar to my parents, Steph showed that she loved me while at the never asking for anything in return. Although I'm sure they're out there, I have yet to meet another woman as smart, entertaining, and attractive as Steph who doesn't expect her boyfriend to give them anything in return. Not to say there wasn't things she wanted, she simply never demanded anything which in turn made her that much more adorable and made me want to give her everything I could.

It's amazing how people have the power to make you give them everything you have to offer. They don't have to ask, all they have to do is act natural. But sometimes it's hard to find a way to show that special person what they mean to you. Due to this problem, I wanted to write another book that listed the easiest, cheapest, and most effective ways to show someone you love them. As I was too busy writing my own book, I had my sister Angie write it for me. She's incredibly intelligent, very creative, and is the most frugal person I know, so it was fitting that she wrote this book. If you sign up on www.HelpaKidinLove.com you will receive my newsletter in which you will get one her 365 ideas in your mailbox once a week. Here are two of my favorites:

42 - Hang a Bed Sheet over the Expressway

Effort: Moderate

Price: $7.50

Effectiveness: 4 and a half hearts (out of 5)

I was driving to school one day and hanging from the side of a freeway overpass was a homemade sign made out of what looked to be a bed sheet which had spray painted writing that read, "happy anniversary, I love you Nicole."

How hard is it to come up with $7.50? How much time would it take to hang a bed sheet from the overpass that your loved one drives under every day to work? How much time of your life would this effort consume? Not very much I would think. How big of a message does it send? How happy will Nicole be when she sees that someone took the extra time to tell her he loves her? Not only did he tell her, but he also wasn't afraid to let every other commuter on the busiest freeway in Omaha know how much he loves her. Now that's love.

 # 10 - Send a random E-mail that includes quick 4 line poem, like the following:

Effort: Easy

Price: Free

Effectiveness: 4 hearts

Angie's Poem to Randy:

> Randy is so great.
> To see him, I cannot wait.
> He's on my mind both night and day,
> A good lookin' fellow, I must say.

(Just leaving it simple will make them smile.)

Love does not have to be a world changing action. It does not have to be perfectly planned. It does not have to be something 100% original. It just takes a little bit of time, a little effort, and a little heart. These days, time and effort seem like they are hard to come by. People find ways to cram as much as they can into their busy lives. After putting in the hours of work, after running errands, after working on other projects, after working your second job, after doing this, after doing that, any leftover time and effort available for love can be hard to find.

The day the human population wakes up to find it impossible to find the time and energy to spread a little love and put their heart into at least something they do, will be the day the human population should be very, very worried as they have lost touch of the only thing that's truly important in life. How hard is it to show someone you love them? How hard is it to hang a bed sheet over an expressway? How hard is it to log on to a website and forward one email to all of your friends and family?

The lack of time and effort is not what concerns me the most. I have lived long enough, seen enough, read about, watched in person, and have heard enough stories about small acts of love that took incredibly small amounts of time and effort which give me a great deal of confidence that there is still a wealth of time and effort available to put into feelings of love in today's world.

The one area I see room for improvement today, is to increase the level of sharing these great feelings, and making them easily accessible and more widely known to all of those who have yet to experience love for themselves, or for those who simply need another dose of fresh love to turn their day around, enhance their current relationship, or help them get through a rough and lonely time.

Help a Kid in Love

After you have logged on to my website, you will gain access to the only place on the internet where you can write, review, and rank the best love stories from all around the world. Through helpakidinlove.com, you get the chance to be the judge on whose love story is the most heart-touching, heart-breaking, tear-jerking, or just plain amazing.

These stories will hopefully help others through certain times throughout their relationship. I also hope you will find through these stories, just how big of an impact love can have on peoples' lives. I hope my efforts set a good example for all of those who are looking for someone to lead the way and say, "It doesn't matter what ANYBODY thinks! I am going to love this person no matter what, and I want everyone else in the world to know!" I am going to love Steph no matter what she says or does, and no matter what anybody else thinks. And to top it all off, I don't expect her to do anything for me in return.

Through making this commitment, I have also discovered that it makes it so much easier to have the same attitude towards all people in general. Of course it is a different kind of love than what I have for Steph. But when I see someone on the street I now have absolutely no problem having general love for mere strangers even before I meet them. There is next to nothing they can do to keep me from at least caring about them. People make mistakes, people make judgments quickly, people are often unaware of their rudeness, they may be purposely inconsiderate, and are often impolite. Whether intentional or not, the list could go on and on. But the one thing that conquers any fault or imperfection, overcomes all of the defects that we as human population posses, is absolute love. Whether it is the person who checked out your groceries and was just having a bad day or the person who stole the radio and slashed a tire on my car last week, no matter who they are or what they do cannot change the fact that one may still love them.

Speaking of my car burglary, I wish I would have been there when they were breaking into my car. When I was mentioning the break-in to my friend he mentioned how bad he would have beaten the living daylights out of them if he had the chance. I too wanted to meet them very badly, but for a completely different reason. If I would have been there, I could have made a difference to whomever it was that was desperate enough to steal a $200 radio. I thought it was hilarious that they decided to steal a radio that might be worth $200, when there were two books sitting on the passenger seat that are worth millions. They took my radio, but they left the books, *Rule #1* by Phil Town and *Good to Great* by Jim Collins just sitting on the passenger seat. If they only knew about all the magic that sat in that passenger seat, (in the present and in the past) maybe they wouldn't be breaking into other peoples' cars.

Or even better yet, if I could have caught them in the act, I could have asked them if they've ever experienced absolute love before. If not, I could have given them my book and introduced them to my parents and Steph and I could have personally shown them how much better life is when you know and understand what absolute love is like. Maybe they wouldn't have had the desire or capacity to understand absolute love. Maybe I would have had a difficult time explaining it to them or trying to convince them how great it is. If there were problems explaining to a petty thief what absolute love is, I would turn to my last resort of explaining absolute love. I would have offered to take them skydiving.

It's Like Jumping Out of a Plane!

"Life is a daring adventure or nothing at all."
- Helen Keller

Within the last year, I took up the great sport of skydiving. Yes, skydiving is actually a sport! It's not just something crazy you do once in a lifetime. Next to love, it's the most incredible experience life has to offer. It's ironic that both skydiving and love involve *"falling."* There are many other metaphors within skydiving that have helped me understand love and life in general.

There are essentially three basic steps to skydiving:

1 - LOOK UP!
2 - LET GO!
3 - HAVE FAITH!

After you go through a thorough training sequence and learn everything you need to know to jump out of a plane on your own, you are packed into a small plane with other jumpers like sardines as you are about to have the time of your life. It strikes a few nerves in you when you take off as all you can think about is how you are going to get back to the ground. When you finally reach a high enough altitude in the plane and once the plane approaches the jump point, your instructor turns a handle and the side door of the plane flies open in a flurry.

You would think that falling is the scariest part of skydiving, but I learned it is the baby steps you take to get out of the plane that are the most frightening. As the door flies open and as the instructor sees the plane is flying at the right speed, he yells as you can barely hear over the rush of wind, "CLIMB ALL THE WAY OUT!" So here you are, climbing ALL the way out of a plane that is thousands of feet above the ground! You are crouched on your knees in order to fit in the cramped plane and you are required to inch your way out of the door.

Right outside the door, just above the landing gear, there is a platform about the size of a piece of paper. When you put your first foot on the platform, you have to look down to make sure that your foot is squarely and firmly planted on the platform and you can do nothing but look at how far down you're about to fall. Once you get the first foot out the door, you have to take baby steps with the rest of your body and eventually you find yourself dangling from the brace which holds up the wing. Your clenched hands are the only things that are keeping you attached to the plane while your legs are just flowing in the wind. Once you're situated on the wing, your instructor points at you and yells the only two words you ever need to hear to accomplish anything in your life.

You can take this as literally or as spiritually as you choose, but it means so many different things at once when he tells you to "LOOK UP!" From a technical perspective, when you look up, your body forms a natural arching position that produces a stable jump. From a psychological perspective, you have more confidence with your chin up. From a spiritual perspective, when you look up, you are doing so in search for strength from above.

When you look up, the next step you are trained to take is to LET GO! They train you so well that the words look up are immediately followed by let go. It happens one after the other like an instantaneous chain reaction. Letting go becomes very easy to do, but cannot be accomplished so easily without first looking up. Before you can let go of the wing, you must learn the proper technique, have confidence, and also look to the heavens to give you strength to immediately let go after you look up.

Once you let go, the only thing stopping you from hitting the ground at 120 mph is a small backpack that contains a parachute that someone else packed for you. Knowing this and letting go requires a great deal of trust in other people. HAVE FAITH! This is the last step listed, but in actuality is required during the entire process. You have to have faith that the people who trained you knew what they were talking about, you have to have faith that the equipment was rigged properly, you have to have faith in the pilot, and most importantly you have to have faith in yourself. Once you are finally freefalling at 120 mph, you just simply have to have faith, just for faith's sake.

The way I see the process is something as follows:

Look Up! – Something's got to be up there
Let Go! – Leave all your worries behind
Have Faith! – It's all going to work out just fine

The great thing about skydiving is that there are all kinds of people within the sport who have no reservations of telling you how great the experience is. They go to great lengths to help you prepare for your jump so you can enjoy it as much as they did without getting hurt. Besides free falling at 120 mph, skydivers enjoy doing two things more than anything else. They like to talk about how great their most recent jump was, and they like to teach others how to do the same. They can't wait to tell the whole world what it's like.

Why don't most people in love have the same mindset? Why is it that most people keep the feeling of love to themselves? I have jumped out of a plane with nothing but a small backpack strapped to my back and a view from the plane like no other. It was one of the most amazing experiences I have been through. The freefall was like paradise in the sky. Being in absolute love is much harder to describe, but the feeling of falling at 120mph with nothing but a backpack strapped to your back only provides a fraction of the excitement and incredible rush of emotions that love can bring.

I would do anything to be in the place of love that I found myself with Steph. But before anything happens again with anyone, I have to remind myself that I will always have some type of support system, a parachute of sorts, to catch my fall. Love is just as dangerous as skydiving. It requires the same mindset, requires you to look up, let go, and have faith. It also requires a support system that is there to cushion the fall. In skydiving, you are as good as dead if the first and the second parachutes fail to open properly. In love, you are in the same predicament without a support system when someone so perfect comes along and all of a sudden forces you to let go.

For obvious reasons, I am glad I get to wear a parachute every time I jump out of a plane. For not-so-obvious reasons, I am extremely lucky to have loving parents, two sweet grandmothers, a church to go to, good books to read, friends to be with, a university to attend, and music to listen to. My support system for life is just like a skydiver's parachute. Without my support system, I might have had to resort to some other kind of parachute. Drugs, alcohol, violence, self-pity, anger, and frustration are all plausible alternatives for a support system if there is no loving family, no congregation of faith, no good books to read, and no education to fall back on. Another conceivable alternative is suicide. Why bother looking for a parachute at all? Jumping out of a plane without a parachute would be equally destructive as losing a loved one without at least some type of support system.

If you are looking for a support system; if you would like to fall back on something other than anger, frustration, drugs, or alcohol, please log on to my website (www.HelpaKidinLove.com) and ask the world to help you cushion your fall. Personally, I may not understand what you are going through. This book may not be able to solve all your problems, but if you post your story on my site, and let other people in the world know what you're going through, there is a very good chance that someone else will come across your story that has experienced something similar and can relate to your situation and help you out.

Let the world be your support system. I would be happy to lend you a better parachute than what you may or may not have right now. On the other hand, if you realize you already have a good support system, if you know your parachute is packed and ready to go, by all means, jump out of that plane! Fall in love! Just do it! Carpe Diem! Memento Mori! Look up! Let Go! Have Faith!

Life and love could learn a lot from the sport of skydiving. Each step is equally important whether it be skydiving, love, your faith, your business, your profession, or just life in general. In some cases it is more literal than others, but by following the simple steps of looking up, letting go, and having faith can help you get through any part of your life.

Just always remember to:

Look Up! – Something's got to be up there

Let Go! – Leave all your worries behind

Have Faith! – It's all going to work out just fine

Telling Everyone about Your Jump

When you finally hit the ground, even if it hurts a little bit, tell the entire world about your jump. Do you love someone absolutely? Tell whoever it is you're thinking about that you love them. Stop, put the book down, tell them in person, call them on the phone, if they're no longer living, send up a prayer, but either way tell that one person that means more than anything in your life that you love them. If it's absolute, don't just say "I love you." Say "I love you, absolutely!"

Now, after you tell that person you love them, tell the whole world! Tell your neighbors, tell your friends, tell your family members. Send emails, text messages, flash hand signals, write it in brail, and whatever else you can think of. You could even do what I did. Write a book, start a website, or just log on to mine, I've already done the work for you so you can electronically tell millions of people who you love. Put up a sign that says you love them, and start walking around the neighborhood telling everyone you meet that you love one certain someone.

Even if your relationship is going just fine, even if you're thinking to yourself, "I'm not the type of person who wants to tell everyone I love a special someone," please reconsider sharing your story with others. Besides myself, there are millions of people who could learn something from you, especially if you're one of the lucky ones to have a relationship still going strong.

You can share your valuable story by logging onto my website. On the website you can make your love span the entire globe in a matter of days. This website was created simply as a way to share the emotions of love, provide examples for others to learn from, and most importantly provide feedback to anyone looking for advice. If you've been lucky enough to be in love whether you've been through a heart-breaking struggle or not, you can share your experience and knowledge of love with millions of people who could learn a lot from what you've been through. You could even start your own webpage if you would like, but I warn you, it takes a lot of work to get it just right. Maybe I've gone a little overboard here, but I hope you get my point. If you've been lucky enough to feel absolute love, or even if you've experienced general love, even for a split second, do whatever is required to let as many people know what it feels like. It's your duty.

Tell them it's better than skydiving!

Help a Kid in Love

Chapter 8

One Who Has Loved Truly, Can Never Lose Entirely

Q: What if you're in absolute love and you lose?
A: YOU CAN'T LOSE!

> "Sometimes you have to hit the bottom
> before you can reach the top."

No one knows how far how you have to go to get to the point where you can declare that you've hit bottom. It just might be possible that when you truly and absolutely love someone that there simply is no bottom. If it is real, if you have truly fallen in love to the deepest degree, wouldn't it make sense that you could just keep falling until the end of time?

Moving on requires you to reach a point where you become fed up with hopelessly falling and drives you to use your emotions to propel you to the top.

The great thing about absolute love is that it is so powerful, it never leaves. Lingering love, especially unrequited, might sound more painful than great, but I have learned that the lingering feelings of absolute love, the smoldering remains of the fire, may be reignited and used to your advantage to get yourself back on your feet. If done correctly, you will not only get back on your feet, but you may find yourself in a place far ahead of where you would have been if you had not taken such a hard fall. The words, "one who has loved truly, can never lose entirely," came directly from the book, Think and Grow Rich.

In Napoleon Hill's masterpiece, he fully dissects the emotion of love and hints towards much different advice on how to handle a broken heart. Without his explanation of love, without his method of viewing failures as "equivalent seeds of success," I would have never found myself using my love to write a book. His writing played a large role in helping me (and millions of other people in the world) move on from heart breaking struggles. The author was not an expert on relationship advice. He was an expert on success. If you have yet to read Think and Grow Rich, you are missing out on one of the most powerful, motivating, and inspiring books ever written.

The author spent 20 years of his life (during part of the great depression) interviewing and studying the most successful men and women in America. After studying the likes of Andrew Carnegie, Henry Ford, Thomas Edison, Abraham Lincoln, Theodore Roosevelt, William Jennings Bryan, and many others, he discovered a consistent pattern and common characteristics of all the most successful people in history.

He found that among all the great people in history, the majority experienced great setbacks in their lives before they became as successful as they were. The trick used by many of these successful people involved taking their painful downfall and turning it into a wonderful opportunity. As he says, "Every failure brings with it the seed of an equivalent success." His book gives you the power to get over any so-called failures.

Since broken hearts might possibly be life's most common form of a setback and quite often the most painful, he dedicates an entire chapter to the emotions of love. No one could write it better than Mr. Hill, so I've simply borrowed the important words from his book:

When driven by this desire (love), men develop keenness of imagination, courage, will-power, persistence, and creative ability unknown to them at other times. When harnessed and redirected along other lines, this motivating force maintains all of its attributes of keenness of imagination, courage, etc., which may be used as powerful creative forces in literature, art, or in any other profession or calling. Scientific research has disclosed the significant fact that those who have accumulated great fortunes and achieved outstanding recognition in literature, art, industry, architecture, and the professions, were motivated by the influence of a woman.

(Abraham) Lincoln was a notable example of a great leader who achieved greatness, through the discovery, and use of his faculty of creative imagination. He discovered, and began to use this faculty as the result of the stimulation of love which he experienced after he met Ann Rutledge.

(Not only was Ann his first love, she was also his greatest loss in life. In 1835, a wave of typhoid hit the town of New Salem, Illinois leading to Ann's early death. This sad event left Lincoln severely depressed. You know the rest of the story as Lincoln goes on to become one of the greatest presidents of

United States history, abolishing slavery and is often referred to as "the great emancipator." Not too shabby for having to first go through life's most painful experience.)

Napoleon Bonaparte was inspired by his first wife, Josephine, and was irresistible and invincible. When his "better judgment" of reasoning faculty prompted him to put Josephine aside, he began to decline.

(Napoleon was imprisoned and then exiled to the island of Saint Helena. Sick for much of his time on the small island, Napoleon died on May 5th, 1821. His last words were: "France, the Army, head of the Army, Josephine.")

Find, if you can, a single man, in all history of civilization, who achieved outstanding success in any calling, who was not driven by a well developed (understanding and experience of love.) The desire for (feelings of love) are by far the strongest and most impelling of all human emotions, and for this very reason this desire, when harnessed and transmuted into action, other than that of physical expression, may raise one to the status of genius. The world is ruled, and the destiny of civilization is established, by the human emotions.

(With love being the most powerful emotion, it would be fair to say that the world is ultimately ruled, and the future of mankind is in the end determined by the wonderful emotions of love.)

When the emotion of love (is understood) the result is calmness of purpose, poise, accuracy of judgment, and balance. Love is the emotion which serves as a safety valve, and insures balance, poise, and constructive effort. Encourage the presence of these emotions as the dominating thoughts in one's mind, and discourage the presence of all the destructive emotions.

The emotion of love softens, modifies, and beautifies the facial expression. It leaves its impress upon one's very soul, even after the fire has been subdued by time and circumstance. Memories of love never pass. They linger, guide, and influence long after the source of stimulation has faded. There is nothing new in this. Every person, who has been moved by genuine love, knows that it leaves enduring traces upon the human heart. The effect of love endures, because love is spiritual in nature. The man who cannot be stimulated to great heights of achievement by love, is hopeless—he is dead, though he may seem to live.

The major force of love may spend itself and pass away, like a fire which has burned itself out, but it leaves behind indelible marks as evidence that it passed that way. Its departure often prepares the human heart for a still greater love. Go back into your yesterdays, at times, and bathe your mind in the beautiful memories of past love. It will soften the influence of the present worries and annoyances. If you believe yourself unfortunate, because you have "loved and lost," perish the thought. One who has loved truly, can never lose entirely.

Love is whimsical and temperamental. Its nature is ephemeral, and transitory. It comes when it pleases, and goes away without warning. Accept and enjoy it while it remains, but spend no time worrying about its departure. Worry will never bring it back.

Dismiss, also, the thought that love never comes but once. There may be, and there usually is, one love experience which leaves a deeper imprint on the human heart than all the others, but all love experiences are beneficial, except to the person who becomes resentful and cynical when loves makes its departure. There should be no disappointment over love, and there would be none if people understood the emotions of love. No experience, which touches the human heart with a spiritual force, can possibly be harmful, except through ignorance, or jealousy.

Love is, without question, life's greatest experience.

Get Over it?

I don't understand the term "get over it." It just doesn't make sense. First of all what is there to get over? If it was true, absolute love there is nothing to get over, only things to remember and in a sense, celebrate. Secondly, if there was such a way to get over being so in love, why would you want to do it in the first place? As you just read Napoleon Hill's description of love, you should start beginning to see that love is something wonderful, something powerful, and something you should be using to your advantage, NOT trying to *get over.*

Being in absolute love is the most powerful, wonderful, and motivating emotion you will ever experience. Why should you try get rid of such an emotion? Rather than dispelling it, why not redirect it? Why not use that same energy and passion to do something else with your life. It is possible to keep those feelings around and keep them at bay before you find someone else to love. There is no need to try to *hide* feelings of love. The secret to using your emotions and the best solution to a broken heart involves redirecting or *transmuting* these feelings.

The way I see it, feelings of love are like diamonds in the rough. Your life, if it is at all similar to mine, is usually never completely perfect. But there are times in your life, times when you're in love, times when it seems like everything is going so perfect, and times it feels like you're walking in the clouds. These times and these memories of love are the diamonds of your past. Common relationship advice tries to convince you to sweep these diamonds under the rug like a pile of dust and forget about them. My advice, which I can personally attest to its effectiveness, is to *not* sweep your sparkling memories under a rug. If you really want to become something great, if you want some incredible things to happen in your life, pick up your diamonds, dust them off, put them on a shelf, and just stare at them for awhile. Don't ever forget about those diamonds. Don't forget what they did for you, don't forget how you arrived at getting them in the first place, and don't ever forget that there are plenty more diamonds left for you to uncover in your future.

You can use your diamonds as stepping stones, taking you from one great love to the next. You don't have to get over anything. You just have to appreciate what you were given, and then look up, let go, and have faith that something even greater is bound to happen in your life. Accept and welcome the reality that relationships don't last forever. Enjoy the ride. Steph always says, "Life is too short to be anything but happy."

Often, people's hardest struggles are their most treasured memories, and their toughest life experiences are time and time again their greatest teachers of life.

> *"Things don't go wrong and break your heart*
> *so you can become bitter and give up.*
> *They happen to break you down and build you up*
> *so you can be all that you were intended to be."*
>
> \- Charles "Tremendous" Jones

Unrequited Love

Before I get into fully describing how you can love your way through a heartache, unrequited love must be completely understood. The ultimate goal here is to get you to "fall out" of unrequited love if you so desire. Getting someone to stop loving unrequitedly does not mean they have to completely stop loving that special someone altogether. Don't forget about the nine other types of love. Even after getting through the pain of unrequited love, you will still love them. It may be familial love, religious love, or true love. There will more than likely always be a loving associating with this person. It will now simply take on a different form.

Unrequited love *is love that is not reciprocated, even though reciprocation is deeply desired. This can lead to feelings such as depression, anxiety, and mood swings such as swift changes between depression and euphoria.*

(From Wikipedia.com)

Before trying to get out of the feeling of loving unrequitedly, one should stop and appreciate what unrequited love has accomplished throughout the pages of time. Incredible works or art, literature, and many other professions were the offspring of unrequited love.

One of the greatest poets to ever live was driven by this type love. Dante Alighieri, simply known as Dante, wrote "La Vita Nuova" which means "The New Life" and also wrote *The Divine Comedy* which contains the popular, *Dante's Inferno*. In the beginning of "La Vita Nuova," Dante mentions he intends to write "that which has never been written of any woman." If you take the time to read his amazing poetic description of his beloved Beatrice, you will have no doubts he achieved what he intended to do.

Dante went on the write *The Divine Comedy* in the early 1300's. <u>This epic poem is considered to be the first great works of the Renaissance</u>. Please go back and read the underlined sentence a few more times to fully appreciate what it said. The Renaissance was one the most historical steps mankind has ever taken and Dante's Divine Comedy was the first product of this great movement. The story goes that every single word Dante wrote was inspired by his forever enduring love for his dear Beatrice who never loved him back the way he loved her. In *The Divine Comedy*, Beatrice is described as Dante's guide to heaven as he passes through hell (Inferno), purgatory (Purgatrio), and finally reaches heaven (Paradiso) where his love is his guide to eternal bliss.

His works were so magical, that it led others to study and discover all the nuances of love that were never before considered. Dante can be referred to as the founding father of modern love and was a catalyst to one of the greatest times in human history. The most amazing thing of the whole story is that one of the greatest literary works of all time and the bulk of the Italian Renaissance was started not by a great poet and a great man but by an eight year old girl by the name of Beatrice.

Not only was one of the most epic poems, but also what is often acclaimed, "the greatest works of fiction" written about unrequited love. *Don Quixote* is a Spanish literature masterpiece that tells the story of a man who aspires to become a knight in shining armor fighting for his adored lady, Dulcinea. Although he never even actually sees her, Don Quixote imagines her to be the most beautiful of all women. Quixote, blindly in love, ignores the fact that she is actually a peasant in his home town. It is not important that they never meet in person, but it is the image of Dulcinea being the fuel for Quixote's journey that is ultimately important. Today, Dulcinea is a term used to label objects of unrequited love and implies hopeless devotion and love for a woman. As an example, I *could* say, "Steph is my Dulcinea."

Other great literary works related to the subject of unrequited love include Shakespeare's "A Midsummer Night's Dream," Victor Hugo's "Les Misérables," Leroux's "Phantom of the Opera," Charles Dickens' "Great Expectations," and F. Scott Fitzgerald's "The Great Gatsby." Without unrequited love, a large portion of some of the greatest works in all of literature, of all time, would have never materialized.

Even in music you can find so many great songs written about unrequited love. Eric Clapton's "Layla" is probably the most famous. The story of the creation of this song is pure Hollywood drama, but still worth telling. Eric Clapton's Dulcinea for many years was his friend's wife, Patti Boyd. Clapton's long time friend was George Harrison of the Beatles. Patti Boyd entered into the equation when Clapton was having troubles with his heroin addictions. Although Boyd was simply trying to help a friend with a drug problem, Clapton was falling madly in love with her.

The title, "Layla" was inspired by the classical Persian poem, "Layla and Manjun," which tells the story of a Persian moon-princess who was arranged in marriage with the man her father chose as opposed to the man who was madly in love with her. Layla, performed by Derek and the Dominos (Clapton's band), was part of an album that has been listed as one of the top 100 rock albums of all time.

The point to be made here is that although unrequited love is painful and agonizing, sometimes it produces things of extreme beauty and elegance. It can be, and often is, the fuel for masterpieces. So maybe, before moving on, you might decide to stay in unrequited love as the pain will be worth going through as you create something special. However, if you would prefer moving on, the suggestion I offer is much different from anyone else's advice.

Love Your Way through a Heartache

*"Love is never lost. If not reciprocated,
it will flow back and soften and purify the heart."*

- Washington Irving

Patience is not my specialty, so the suggestion that time will heal the pain does not apply to me. Besides my impatience, all the time in the world wouldn't help me in my situation. Everything was just too perfect to even begin thinking about just sitting around waiting for time to make everything better. I'm sure there are many others out there who feel the same way. This was a situation Napoleon Hill describes as the *"one love experience which leaves a deeper imprint on the human heart than all the others."* This isn't something time will heal, and it is most definitely something I will always remember. Therefore, the best solution is simple: Stop fighting and keep loving.

I spent nearly a year trying everything everyone else recommends. Sure, go ahead, do something constructive, make new friends, try something that you've always wanted to do, go skydiving, go on a few dates, you name it, I tried it. But no matter what I tried, no matter what I did, I always came back to wear I started, in love with Steph.

Eventually love won. One day I sat down and said to myself, "You know what, I'm always going to love this girl no matter what happens, so why am I wasting my time trying to *get over* her?" Ever since I faced the brutal facts, everything has been just as great (some days even better) than the best days when we were together. Because I don't have to *try* to forget something, because I don't have to deny my heart from feeling the way it wants to feel, and because it still gets to be in love with who it wants to be, now the rest of myself feels like it can finally move on.

By keeping your mind and your heart open and letting these feelings of love roam freely, you can enjoy the rest of your life without having to go through the painstaking struggles of trying to forget about that special someone. By recognizing that you love this person, and always will, you can start focusing on all the great opportunities life has to offer rather than zoning in on the problems.

So what they don't love you back? There's nothing stopping you from loving them. I know it's hard when it's not exactly the same as it was before the separation. Whenever I'm driving in my car, there's always an empty feeling wishing there was a cute blond hair girl sitting in my passenger seat trying to take my eyes off the road. I always smile when I think of that bobble-head doll wave, I'll never forget the way she laughs, and I'll always see her big beautiful smile in the back of my mind. She left an indelible imprint on my heart, and it's never going to fade away.

But once you give in, once you surrender, once you stop trying to fight love, you can begin using it. The sole reason for keeping the feelings of love around are for the purpose of redirecting them to do something great with your life. My choice was to write a book and create a website. Other people have built memorials, created libraries, started charities, and accomplished many other wonderful things to benefit society even though their loss was tough. Abraham

Lincoln used his love to rid the nation of slavery, while Napoleon Bonaparte chose to let power to go to his head rather than letting love flow from his heart, and he was defeated twice before passing away in exile.

The difference between Lincoln and Napoleon highlights the importance of how *you* choose to play the cards dealt by life. Lincoln chose to use his emotions for the good of mankind by improving the lives of countless numbers of men and women in America and is forever known as "honest Abe," while Napoleon made the statement, "power is my mistress," and chose to use his emotions to end the lives of millions of men all across Europe and is forever known as "a cruel tyrant." Your life is ultimately determined by the choices you make.

"There is a choice you have to make,
in everything you do.
So keep in mind that in the end,
the choice you make, makes you."

- Anonymous

Again, choosing to use your love applies to any type of setback, be it a break-up, divorce, or even death. Your love, whether returned or not, can be used to enhance your own life as well as the lives of many others in the world. The trick, and often the hard part, is finding a way to transmute your emotions to something other than the one you love. This may be a very sensitive subject depending on your situation, but if you can find something to redirect your love to, especially something that improves the lives of other people, you will find serenity in your heart and peace in your mind. It all revolves around what you choose to attach your feelings to.

Love is often labeled as a bridge of emotions, an invisible, but incredibly powerful union of two people. When that connection is broken through separation, divorce, or death, the bridge of love still remains. Not only does it stay standing, sometimes it stands stronger when the other end of the bridge suddenly disappears. Common relationship advice often tells you to try to tear down the bridge piece by piece until you are ready to start building your bridge all over again. "Take baby steps, time will heal your pain," is the overarching message most people preach.

I can see the logic behind the point of view that most people have on getting over relationships, and I appreciate what other "experts" on love, relationships, and psychology have written. However, I would like to ask one important question: Did they write their books about getting through tough situations while they were actually in them? Again, I realize that I'm just a 21 year-old and still have a lot to learn about both life and love. I'm not saying that one way is better than another or that it's not as meaningful writing about theoretical situations. It just irritates me that no one ever mentioned to me that it would be much easier and much more effective if I just kept on loving her.

Keep the bridge up! Just find something else to connect it to. Take the same wonderful emotions and attach them to starting a business, writing a book, building a webpage, abolishing slavery, or a million other things you could do in memory of someone you love. I pray that you respect the power of love and use it for the good of mankind rather than trying to dispel it and going through the pain of forgetting about it. When you choose to use the feelings of love to your advantage, when you put as much effort and attention to something constructive, you might surprise yourself with the results.

Begin pursuing your life long dreams, and start living! But don't stop loving. If done with the memories of love in mind, you will witness incredible things being done as you will leave everything you have to offer in life all on the table. Leaving everything on the table is another step which will help you escape unrequited love. It is also something not usually mentioned in relationship books. What is meant by "leaving it all on the table," is that you do everything you can think of to show someone you love them. By giving your special someone everything you have to offer you will find it much easier to walk away without expecting, demanding, or even wishing for anything in return.

The difficult, but required part, involves you doing so without being a pest. I could have called up Steph everyday and begged her to listen to me tell her how much I love her, but instead I decided to write a book and let her read it at her discretion. Now that I wrote a book that completely describes how I feel about her, and by giving her this book that provides a guide to help her get through life's toughest situations, there's nothing I haven't written that I want her to know. I'm not going to *make* her read it, but at least I know it's there, just in case. I never have to wake up someday and ask myself, "What if?"

When someone who once loved you very passionately no longer does, you are given two options. You can either expect them to love you back and throw your temper tantrums, or you can continue to love them no matter what, with absolutely no expectations. If the second option is your choice, than you can say you truly love that person and you will have no problem moving on. However, if you feel like you deserve something, if you feel they're obligated to do something or give something more to you, if you think you've been "done wrong," maybe you should rethink whether you really love this person or that you are lusting out of infatuation and you're not, and never were, truly in love.

  More than likely, there will be no explanations and no reasons. Even if it was your fault for the relationship ending, you may have no way to explain why it all happened the way it did. That is what makes it so tough. No one can explain *why* it had to end, it just did. It's so hard to go through the changes when all you would like to know is "Why!?" But, once you have reached the point where you hold no expectations, desire no answers, and just accept what you're dealt with, the pain of the absence of reciprocation will vanish. When there is no longer a desire for reciprocation, if you're happy with loving someone with no wishes or demands that they do the same, it can no longer be labeled unrequited love. Part of the definition of unrequited love includes reciprocation being deeply desired. If you have no demands for the love to come full circle, if you continue to love with no expectations, then you have successfully left the painful realm of unrequited love.

Stop Preventing Death and Start Promoting Life

*"Every man dies,
not every man really lives."*

- William Wallace (Braveheart)

Do you have a list of things you want to accomplish in life? Are you taking active steps in pursuing them? After Steph broke up with me, I had a lot of time to think about things and determine what I wanted out of life. Because she was my biggest dream that I wanted to come true, I saw no reason why any others couldn't. Before getting the chance to be with Steph, I was pursuing the same goals as the majority of people by striving for society's general consensus of dreams. Before Steph, if I made a list of the things in life I was taking active steps to achieve, it would have been three items long:

1. Get a college diploma
2. Find someone to fall in love with
3. Support my family with a good job

Not to say that it is a poor list by any standards, but it seriously lacks creativity and imagination. A few moths after she broke up with me, I was playing basketball with some of my friends. After the pickup games were over, my friends were all ready to leave the gym as I was hopelessly trying to put it down, just once, one clean dunk, that's all I wanted. I didn't need to be the next Michael Jordan. I just wanted to be able to say that I dunked it once in my lifetime. My friends were sitting on the end of the stage on the opposite side of the gym, ready to leave, as I made another one of my thousands of attempts of a clean dunk. Ever since my freshman year in high school (when I was 5'6" and 135 lbs) I've been trying to dunk a basketball on a regulation hoop. I remember as an eighth-grader, betting my older brother ten dollars that I would dunk it at least once before I graduated. Seven years, four inches of vertical growth, and one lost bet later; something I expected (and no one else did) happened. It went down! Cleanly! And best of all, my friends saw it! I had witnesses! I had proof! It took over seven years and thousands of attempts to finally get it down, but I did it! And it didn't stop at one time. I did it again, and again, and again. Now it was like riding a bike.

When I got home that night I thought to myself, if I'm lucky enough to get the chance to be with Steph, if a 5'10" scrawny white kid from Nebraska can dunk it, what other cool things could I do? The only requirement to achieve all your dreams is effort. All you have to do is try, try, and try some more, and eventually something magical happens. That night I chose to actually create a list of things I wanted to do in life. A list of things no one else has ever written down, and just like my dream of being able to dunk a basketball on a regulation size hoop, I'm sure no one else (other than me) expects them to materialize.

Things I Want to do in Life

1. ~~Go on a Date With Steph~~
2. ~~Cleanly Dunk a Basketball on a Regulation Hoop~~
3. ~~Go Skydiving~~

Help a Kid in Love

4. ~~See the Ocean, Go Surfing~~
5. Tell the *Entire* World that I Love Steph
6. Fall in Love, One More Time
    (or as many times as needed)
7. Retire Before I Graduate
    (Coming Soon: www.retirebeforeyougraduate.com)
8. Buy a Brand New Corvette Someday (with cash)
9. Learn to Fly a Plane
10. Run a Full Marathon
11. If #6 Doesn't Happen by Age 57,
    Call "You-Know-Who"

This time the list was much more specific and much more valuable, much more creative, and much more imaginative. And it gets longer and longer all the time as I find cool new things I can do as I cross off each item one by one. I get closer and closer to each new item on the list as long as I never forget about the original reason they all started happening in the first place. Because I always have been and always will be in love Steph; furthermore, because I don't try to hide it or cover it up, any dream I have can come true. After all, it was because I loved her so much that allowed dream #1 to come true. Now she's making all the other dreams come true too. Maybe you're thinking that some of the items could never be accomplished, maybe you are thoroughly convinced that I'm out of my mind. But then again if you would have told me ten years ago that someday Steph would be in love with me, that I would be able to cleanly dunk a basketball, and that I'd be jumping out of planes, I would have thought you were a little crazy too!

If you would like to create a list like mine, I have two suggestions. First make it custom to your passions. Do you really want to do these things? Why do you want to do them? If they're really good ideas, if they're aligned with your desires, you won't have time to ask "why," as you will be spending all of your time asking yourself "how?"

The second suggestion is to start the list with big goals that you've already accomplished so you can begin checking something off immediately. Creating a list with big, hairy, audacious goals that are already completed is the third most motivating source you will find in life.

The second most motivating force in life is *not* having any completed BHAG's to call your own. It's even better if you *can't* think of any big dreams that you've accomplished. Do you want to live your entire life with no accomplished dreams to call your own? If you answered no, if you want to make your life worthwhile, all you need to do is think of just one goal, one dream, one big, hairy, audacious goal. Make your list one item long. Write down that one goal, list three reasons why you want to strive for it, and think of five different ways of how you can achieve it. Post you BHAG somewhere you can always see it and make that the dominating thought of your life. That one goal should be all you think about. One other important step is to tell everyone you know and everyone who might care about your big dreams. Your future, your outlook, and all your dreams of tomorrow depend upon this one goal. Don't think about anything else. Stop doing anything that gets in your way of reaching this all important goal and start taking the small steps of man and strive to help mankind take gigantic leaps and bounds!

Creating a list with big, hairy, audacious goals that are already completed is the third most motivating source you will find in life and *not* yet having any BHAG's to call your own is the second. If you haven't figured this out on your own yet, the greatest motivating force on earth is a man's desire to please a woman or a woman's desire to make a man happy. It all starts with love. Four letters, one word, one emotion has brought forth millions upon millions of great accomplishments. Countless heartbreaks, many emotional setbacks, creations of pure beauty and elegance, and most importantly memories of love that will never pass are all byproducts that begin and end with what is found in the depths of your heart and that which runs throughout your entire soul.

When You Dream, Dream Big

So many people don't allow themselves to dream big, and I think that's a tragedy. Without big dreams, the human population would not be where we are today. Without big dreams, Christopher Columbus would have never discovered the Americas and I'd be living somewhere in Germany, not Nebraska. Without big dreams, Neil Armstrong would have never taken his one small step, and mankind would have never taken its one gigantic leap. If John F. Kennedy never pursued his big, hairy, audacious goal of strapping a human being to a multistage liquid-fuel expendable moon rocket equipped with engines that disperse a total of nearly nine million foot-pounds of force powerful enough to send tremors through the ground that could be felt fifty miles away; if JFK was too afraid to put his dreams into action, mankind would not be able to look up at the moon and say, "Yeah, we've been there."

When all the great astronauts of the world were sitting in their cramped compartments at the top of one of the most impressive and potentially destructive machines in human history, do you think they were trying to calculate the risks they were taking versus the rewards they may or may not receive? Although I'm sure the question of "why" crossed the minds of these great men, it is obvious that they spent more time trying to answer the "how" of the challenge rather than the "why."

(The first Saturn V, AS-501, before the launch of *Apollo 4*)

Help a Kid in Love

If Dr. Martin Luther King Jr. never stood up and proudly declared, "I have a dream," some of my African-American friends from college would still be drinking out of different water fountains than I do. If Charles Babbage would have never sat down one day in 1835, trying to think of a way to get a machine the size of an entire building to compute a few simple math problems, we wouldn't even know what a computer is, let alone be using the power of the internet to tell the *entire* world who we love.

If you're ever going through hard times in your life, if you're ever at a point where you're a little bit (or even very) scared of taking on a big challenge, if you can feel something inside of you that's trying to hold you back, just stop and think about the men who sat atop the rockets that were launched to the moon. Think about Dr. Martin Luther King Jr. and the courage he needed to do all the wonderful things that changed the world. Think about Abraham Lincoln, having to see his beloved Ann pass away and what he *chose* to do afterwards. Most importantly, think about yourself and ask, "Why *shouldn't* I be dreaming big?" Whether it's writing a book, starting a business, or asking someone out on a date, just ask yourself, "why not?"

One of Steph's favorite songs (and one of mine too) addresses the concerns for the lack of dreaming big. This song was released while we were still dating, and it always reminds me of all the wonderful things that happened because of her. Not only does it remind me of all the great things that happen when you dream big, it also serves as the perfect song to help you get through the toughest times in your life.

Chris Miller

Dream Big

And when you cry, be sure to dry your eyes,
'Cause better days are sure to come.
And when you smile, be sure to smile wide,
And don't let them know that they have won.
And when you walk, walk with pride:
don't show the hurt inside,
Because the pain will soon be gone.

When you dream, dream big,
As big as the ocean, blue.
Because when you dream it might come true.
But when you dream, dream big.

And when you laugh, be sure to laugh out loud,
'Cause it will carry all your cares away.
And when you see, see the beauty all around and in yourself,
And it will help you feel okay.
And when you pray, pray for strength to help you carry on,
when the troubles come your way.

And when you dream, dream big,
As big as the ocean, blue.
Because when you dream it might come true.
But when you dream, dream big.

(Lyrics compliments of Ryan Shupe)

Help a Kid in Love

Paint Your Imperfect Masterpiece

I admire the song, "Dream Big," but I disagree with the part in the beginning. Go ahead and dry your eyes and smile wide, but I think you should let them know that they *have* won, and you should *use* the hurt inside rather than trying to hide it. If you do, the pain will not go away, but it will soon feel good, very good.

If you were truly and absolutely in love, why should you be mourning it? If anything, you should be celebrating. This may sound like an odd analogy, but the way I see it is that my relationship with Steph was similar to the basketball game of my life, and no different than the best track meet of my running career. I gave it my all, enjoyed the ride, and can look back at our relationship, smile, and say, "wow, that's what it's like!" This is what life is like when you absolutely, completely, and undeniably love someone and go to the greatest lengths to give them everything you have to offer. Once you do that, you find a way to dig a little bit deeper and give them something more just to make sure you gave them your absolute best. Steph got the absolute best from me, and for that I am satisfied and happy.

Every basketball game I ever played, the clock eventually ticked its way down to zero. Every race I ever ran had a finish line at the end. There were times I wasn't the first to cross the finish line, times we didn't win the game, times I didn't get the shining trophy or gold medal, but knowing I made my greatest possible effort allows me to live my life with no regrets. So what she broke my heart? So what the time ran out in the last basketball game of my career and we lost by three points? So what there has to be a finish line at the State Track Meet? The end is not what's important. It is the ride that gets you there. The journey, the pursuit, the effort put forth, the joy in the moment, the thrill of the start, the perseverance during the rough times, through and through until, as Steve Prefontaine would say, *"there's absolutely nothing left!"* No matter the results, no matter how painful the heartache, it is the experience and the choice of how it is handled that makes us who we are today.

You have a blank canvas in front of you and it's called your future. Depending on your religious beliefs, it is likely this is your first, and only, shot at life. This is your first attempt at "painting a picture," and not to put extra pressure on you, I suggest you paint a masterpiece. Your painting, your life will not be perfect, but if you are able to give it your all, if you are lucky enough to experience absolute love, you will have all you need to paint a masterpiece with life's canvas.

You can let the world around you paint your canvas for you, or you can grab the brush with confidence and produce a masterpiece that is exactly the way you see fit. "Seize the day boys, make your lives extraordinary!" Memento Mori! "Your heart is free, have the courage to follow it." Even if I don't get my happy ending with Steph, even if all 6.5 billion people in the world never find out how much I love her, I know I will be able to look back on my life with no regrets. At any time in the future I can look at what once was a blank canvas, and I will be able to say with self-assurance, "This is my masterpiece."

I am only 21 years-old, but I have learned that life's canvas is not static and stable. It's more like a cotton sheet billowing in the wind. You have to run to catch up with the canvas, and once there, you have to wrestle it to the ground and fervently grind out the ripples as you make adjustments in your life before you even begin trying to paint your picture. But with persistence, you can still create the masterpiece you desire. Sure it won't be absolutely perfect, but it will still display all the requirements of a masterpiece, which are beauty and elegance.

The term "masterpiece" originated from the old European guild system which consisted of journeymen who were aspiring to become master craftsmen. Their pieces of handicraft labeled as masterpieces were admired for their beauty and elegance, and were also their first truly great creation to call their own. If a journeyman tried to produce his masterpiece and failed, there was always hope that his next project would in fact, be his masterpiece. Although you only get one canvas in life, there are millions of opportunities to create your masterpiece. The most important thing to remember is to never give up, never stop moving forward, never stop doing what you love, and *never* forget that you have to follow through.

Follow Through

Creating your chosen masterpiece, redirecting your love to something other than the original source, and ultimately being successful of loving your way through your heartache requires you to set a BHAG, focus on the "how," and prepare yourself to leave it all on the table. Not only should you do everything mentioned thus far, you have to come through on your end of the bargain. You have to follow through.

Hopefully you have replaced the object you desire and are not following through with the wrong pursuit. Hopefully you are not trying to force someone to love you back. If you have in fact redirected and transmuted these powerful emotions, if you've thought of a BHAG that grabs you in the gut and brings the best out of you, if you are beginning to see what your masterpiece might look like, you must take action, and never give up. You can *"build through your destruction"* if you choose to use those *"reeling emotions that keep you alive."* Just make sure it is appropriate to what you're using them for.

"<u>This</u> is the start of something good, don' you agree." Notice that at the end of the song, it is left open as *this*. There is no specific "this" and it can be anything you choose, but no matter what, you're gonna have to follow through. If you truly love someone, you will continue to do so even when they are gone. Whether it is a break-up, divorce, or even death, you will always have the power to choose to love them anyways. No one said you have to stop loving them just because they aren't there anymore or just because they don't love you back. Absolute love is above all and never takes a day off. The most logical thing to do is harness its power, and when done right, your efforts will endure with the power and endurance of the most wonderful and motivating force known to mankind. You will have no choice but to follow through.

Whenever I hear that song, my memory takes me back to my old apartment. I can see how my entire room is laid out, and I can hear Steph in the beginning saying, "You just have to listen to the words." This book is my way of saying in return, "Okay, I'm following through no matter what."

Although I may not see her physically everyday, because I know I love her absolutely and have made the choice not to cover up my feelings for her, I really can see her everyday. She is clearly visible in my thoughts and in my dreams and is the guiding light for all my actions. This is all done without bringing about the hurt of completely forgetting about her. However, at the same time, I have no reserves of being just as committed to the next diamond of my life.

What If?

What if? Depending on their use, the two words, "what if," are by far my favorite words, and can also be my most feared words within the English language. Looking forward, into the future, the words "what if" are so powerful. What if I do something I've always wanted to do? What if I went skydiving? What if I run a marathon? What if I learn to fly a plane? What if I tell the *entire* world that I love Steph? What if this book helps someone get through a difficult time of their life? What if? When you have a positive, forward outlook on life, the words, "what if" are more powerful than any other words which may be spoken.

Looking back on the past, the words "what if" take on a whole new meaning. What if I would have done it differently? What if I would have just followed my heart? What if I had gave just a little more effort? What if I didn't let other people tell me how to live my life? What if I wouldn't have been too afraid? What if I did this? What if I did that? What if! I never want to look back on my life and have to ask myself, "What if?" When I'm an old man, when I look back, I want to be able to say, "Well, it turned out differently than I may have imagined, but I put forth my best effort towards the important things I've always wanted to pursue."

Personally, I think the worst feeling in the world is that of regret. Even if you make mistakes, you can still look at every situation as a learning experience. Everything within human power should be used to dispel regret. From the very beginning, follow your heart, find your treasures, welcome the power and endurance of absolute love, love truly as you can never lose entirely, and follow through… with every word you say.

Help a Kid in Love

Chapter 9

Help a Kid in Love

(Hopefully I've Helped You First)

By now you should have a new view on the subject of a broken heart, and hopefully now have an empathetic (not sympathetic) attitude towards my situation. Again, this book was not written for sympathy, it was simply written to show Steph what she means to me, to show the *entire* world what absolute love is like, and to show the *entire* world the best way to handle a broken heart. If you have vicariously experienced my feelings through this book, if it feels like you just walked a mile in my shoes, then you should be fully aware and completely convinced that I still care about Steph more than anything else in the universe. But in a weird twist of love, those same exact feelings are the basis of what's allowing me to move on.

If you are in a similar situation as me, I truly hope this book will help improve your life in every way imaginable. It is my dream that everyone in the world will have the opportunity to read this book, but more importantly I want to ensure that those who are going through a rocky time in their life get the chance to read it first. If you know of someone you feel that might appreciate this book, please do not hesitate to lend them your book and tell them about my website.

Help a Kid in Love

Even if you do not completely agree with my philosophy, even if you don't feel like my approach is the best way to handle your specific situation, even if this is not the choice you want to make with your life, I still hope that through reading my story you have learned something about the subject of love. Forever am I a student of this wonderful emotion, and I will always be a faithful follower of the one thing that can accomplish so much in this world, but also has the potential to cause such indescribable pain. The curious kid inside me will always be asking, "What is love?" I will always be looking to build something, whether it's a castle built out of Legos or a relationship built on trust, friendship, companionship, compassion, concern, tenderness, sympathy, faith, affection, devotion, and loyalty. And more than likely, I will eventually find myself in a world of hurt. Good thing it is the ride that is worth it, and not the destination; otherwise, I wouldn't know what to do.

Although I offered my advice throughout much of this book, and mentioned the three ultimate reasons for its creation, one other reason, so far untouched, was from the perspective of someone looking to seek help rather than give it. There are plenty of self help books out there on every subject from love, to money, to do it yourself projects, weight loss, and anything else you can imagine. The one subject I could not find a self help book on, was for someone like me who can't stop loving someone, but still wants to move on with their life. Although I feel that I've found the most effective way of doing so, I am still curious to see what the *entire* world thinks about my situation and my philosophy.

Also, I am dying to find out what it takes to make a relationship go the distance. Am I doing something wrong? Do I just need to be more patient? Are there certain characteristics, certain qualities, certain skills that I should look for and develop that will make my relationships (especially the ones that feel so perfect) last as long as I wish? The odds are high that if you don't know what it's like to move on from a broken heart, that you are probably still in a terrific relationship and I would greatly appreciate it if you could stop for a moment, think about why you think it's lasted so long, and share with me what it is that keeps the relationship together. Now that you know the story, and now that you have an idea of just how special Steph is to me, I would appreciate any suggestions or comments about what you think I could do, or what I should do whether regarding her or the next special someone that comes along in my life. I already know what it's like to be with someone who is your best friend and your confidant, but I don't know what it's like to have that feeling stick around as long as it has for my parents, and so many other happy couples in the world. Please log on to my website and find the link that says "Going the Distance," and tell me what you think makes healthy relationships stand the test of time.

I've had many people tell me about their relationships that were very similar to mine with Steph. Some have said they went through almost the exact same thing and after enough time had passed, they happily reunited. Other people have said that changes like this have led them to even better (but different) things in their life. There's no way to tell for sure what will happen, and I don't think there really is a right or wrong thing to do. But nevertheless, I would like to hear your thoughts.

If you've got a similar story, you too can post it on my website. After not only experiencing, but also writing an entire book on broken hearts, I would be especially interested in your story and your point of view if you have ever lost someone you love more than life itself, but have somehow found a way to enjoy life just as much (maybe even more) after you had to let go of this special someone. I would like to know what you did and how your story unfolds. If you have a story to share, please log on to my website and put your thoughts online. To protect your privacy, you can remain completely anonymous if you wish. I recommend spilling your guts and not trying to hide anything because that is what worked for me, but it is completely up to you, just as it is your choice on how to handle a broken heart.

Personally, I feel like I'm moving in the right direction. I still love her. I care for her and want the best for her. However, I would have no problem riding off in the sunset with the next great opportunity that comes along. My method of getting through rough times may be too new to prove effective for everyone, so I advise you to proceed with caution. But if it works for you, please post your story on my webpage. I am curious to know what you have been through in the world of love, what you have gained, what you have lost, and last but not least, what you have learned through all your experiences, good and bad, happy and sad.

Chris Miller

HelpaKidinLove.com

Even though now I have found a way to get through it all, even though I'm moving on, the curiosity inside me still wants to know what you think about my situation. Once you sign up on my main website, I will give you access to another site where you can view my story online and post your feedback. Through this site you can post comments, give advice, participate in polls, and give me and many other users other than myself your valuable feedback. You can also post your own story on this site as you will be able to get the *entire* world's opinion on your situation. You too can use this site to post your own love story and get feedback from the *entire* global community.

You can tell the *entire* world who you love and spill all your guts; or if you wish, you can remain completely anonymous. The best thing about it all is that you get feedback from people who truly care, but are not so close to you that they may say something other than the truth to avoid hurting your feelings. All too often friends and relatives (although caring) do not reveal their true thoughts.

Although the feedback you receive will be extremely beneficial, the information obtained can only be used as a secondary source as you should now be using your primary source, your heart, to make your decisions in life with guidance from your own mind. Every scenario is different and every situation may require a different solution. Just by reading one book alone may not be enough to get you where you want to be, but simply by writing down your thoughts and feelings so others can understand your situation will ultimately help you understand yourself much more. By posting your story online, you also get customized feedback that is specifically tailored to your situation. As the website grows, and as I get more feedback from my story, I will continue to do everything I can to help you in anyway possible. If you can think of anything else I could do to help you out, please let me know. As I have, and will continue to do everything I can think of to help you out, now it is my turn to ask the biggest favor I've ever asked of anyone in my life.

Help Me Tell the *Entire* World!

*"God tends to throw himself
on the side of a man who knows
exactly what he wants,
if he is determined to get just that!"*

- Napoleon Hill

In order for me to create my masterpiece, I'm going to need your help. My big, hairy, audacious goal of telling the *entire* world that I love Steph cannot come true without your help. Spread the word! Chris loves Steph, Pass it on, HelpaKidinLove.com! That's all you have to say. It just takes a few clicks of the mouse and you can easily tell hundreds and hundreds of people. I've listed multiple ways of efficiently telling everyone you know about this mission of making history. Don't forget that if everyone eventually finds their way to my website, your own love story can be exposed to them as well.

Chris Miller

The Goal is Possible!

In the previous chapter, when I was mentioning dreaming big, I wasn't just making that up and saying it because it sounded nice. I believe in it, and if you don't, then that is a red-flag going up that says that you have yet to discover, choose not to recognize, or fail to remember what absolute love is like. Amazing things can truly happen when someone sets their mind *AND* their heart to something. So many people will tell you in your life that you can do anything if you set your mind to it. What they didn't tell you, is that you will not get very far if you don't allow your heart lead the way to what it is that you are setting your mind to. Also, in the very beginning of the book, I mentioned how I could tell the entire world in just a few years and now I would like to reveal to you the simple secrets of how I can tell the *entire* world in an incredibly short period of time. It will take a lot of effort on my part, and just a few clicks of the mouse on your part.

If each day I can convince 25 people on my own to help me achieve my goal, and if these 25 people agree to send the message to 100 people, and if those 100 people also tell 100 people, and those 100 people tell 100 people then in a very short amount of time the *entire* world will know about "Help a Kid in Love."

Help a Kid in Love

Here's how the numbers work:

25 - People per day that I personally get to help me
x 5 – Working days of the week (I read stories and help out others on my website on the weekend.)
x 52 – Weeks in the year
x 100 – People that the first 25 people tell
x 100 – People that the second 100 people tell
x 100 – People that the third 100 people tell
= 6,500,000,000, THE ENTIRE WORLD!

If you do the math, I will have to tell 25 people per day, 125 people per week, and 6,500 people altogether in one year. All you have to do is tell 100 people. You might be thinking that it would take a lot of work to tell 100 people, but in the next few pages I will show you how you can effortlessly tell way more than 100 people something in less than 30 seconds per day, over the course of just one week. Altogether you might spend three and a half minutes throughout the entire week contributing to history in the making. I've made an outline you can follow if you doubt how easy this really is.

How to Tell Everyone You Know in One Week

Help a Kid in Love - 7 Day Checklist

Day 1 - Sign up on HelpaKidinLove.com
    Submit your own story if you'd like
    Tell everyone in your household

Day 2 – Tell all of your email contacts
    Tell all your relatives

Day 3 - Tell all of your co-workers or classmates

Day 4 - Tell everyone in your social community
    Virtual Networks (i.e. Facebook)
    Good Old Fashioned Grapevine

Day 5 - Tell someone nice you meet (HaKiL Card)

Day 6 - Tell a Stranger (Bumper Sticker and T-Shirt)

Day 7 – Tell everyone at your religious gathering place

Day 1

In less than a minute a day we can tell the entire world who we love. Just remember the slogan:

"Chris loves Steph
(or) I Love _____
Pass it on
HelpaKidinLove.com."

If you are near a computer, (and if you have not yet done so) simply visit helpakidinlove.com, submit your email address and if you're at home, while your on my site, ask everyone in your house to come look at the crazy kid on the internet that's trying to tell the *entire* world that he loves one girl. While you're at it, you can sign up and search around on my website, read other people's amazing love stories, or even post your own if you wish to receive feedback. If you simply want to tell the entire world who you love, you can do that as well.

Day 2

Of all seven days, day two requires the least amount of effort. By now you should have received an email from me with the subject: Chris Loves Steph, Pass it on, HelpaKidinLove.com. Open up the email and take a look at the message and forward this to EVERYONE in your contact list. Just click forward, then click all, then send it away. That's all there is to it. How easy was that? You can even write in the forward who you love. Depending on how many people you have in your contact list, you could have just told hundreds of people in a matter of seconds. And if each person you forwarded the message to does the same, very quickly the *entire* world will know about Help a Kid in Love.

If you did not happen to have all of your family members listed in your contact list, I recommend you find out what their email addresses are and forward the message to them as well. It would be a shame if you did not have an easy way to contact all your family members, and it's about time you get updated with their contact information so you can get a hold of them if something else comes along.

Day 3

Are you ever bored at work or in class? Do you ever talk to your co-workers or classmates? As I'm sure you often have some down-time, whether it's a lunch break or just plain slow, and as you hopefully talk to your co-workers or classmates on a day to day basis, why not bring up my mission? Just for fun, ask them if they have heard about my website. If they haven't, I bet you they will be interested and it will give you something exciting to talk about. It sure is better than talking about the weather or complaining about your boss at work or teachers in school.

Day 4

The internet is wonderful. It connects so many people in such an organized and efficient manner. Log on to Facebook, MySpace, or whatever social networking website you use, and search for the group or event called "Help a Kid in Love." If there isn't one on your social network yet, feel free to create one, just don't forget to add a link to HelpaKidinLove.com. On most of these online networks you can invite all of your friends and contacts to join the group or event, and I have provided pictures and instructions if you're not exactly sure what to do.

Facebook

Step 1: Type "Help a Kid in Love" in the search bar (It should pop up on the top of the list) If you can't find the group, search for me (Chris Miller, University of Nebraska Omaha) and you should be able to find the group under my profile.

Step 2: Join the Group

Step 3: Invite ALL of your friends. (See Picture)

Step 4: Send Invitations, and viola!

Help a Kid in Love

Message All Members
Edit Group Profile
Edit Group Members
Edit Group Officers
Invite People to Join
Leave Group

Group Type — edit

This is an open group. Anyone can join and invite others to join.

Admins

- Chris Miller (creator)

Other Virtual Networks

If you log on to wikipedia.com, and type in "list of social networking websites," you can see a list of just about every social networking website that exists. I'm working on getting into each and every one of these networks, and as I go, I will post instructions on my website, that shows how you can spread the word and effectively tell everyone in these networks. If you are currently using a social networking site that I have not yet created a group for, please feel free to create a group/event/message that talks about Help a Kid in Love, just don't forget to include a link to www.HelpaKidinLove.com.

Offline Grapevine

If you're not part of the generation that lives online, if you prefer to stay away from computers altogether, have no fear! I have discovered that the good old fashioned grapevine (talking face to face) is often just as effective as the internet. Besides family and co-workers, tell everyone else you see everyday about my goal. Your dry cleaner, your neighbors, your doctor, dentist, lawyer (yes, lawyers have hearts too), and anyone else you can think of. If you've posted your own story on my website tell them you're trying to tell the entire world who you love. When they ask how you plan to do it, just tell them to go to my website, or tell them about my book. If you just tell them your story (or mine) they will more than likely talk about our goal in many of their next conversations they have, and before you know it, love will span the entire globe!

Day 5

When you sign up online (or if you click on the link on the top right corner of the webpage, "Get the Book") you are redirected to the page where you can purchase my book and where you can also get more tangible Help a Kid in Love stuff. With a donation to my chosen charities you can receive my "HaKiL card" which is a plastic card the size of a credit card. The instructions are provided on the card and the object is simple. You must give this card to someone you care about, but cannot give it back to the person who gave it to you. If each person passes the card to another person each day, just one of these plastic cards has the power to tell at least 365 people and can travel as far as the mind can imagine.

Day 6

When you're on my website, you can purchase a bumper sticker and a T-Shirt that shows everyone that you are helping a kid in love. You have the opportunity to customize the back of the T-Shirt so you could replace the names Chris and Steph with your name and the name of your own special someone. You'd be surprised how many people will stop and talk to you when they see you wearing this shirt.

The money paid for these items goes directly to the costs that were incurred in their production and the majority of any would-be profit goes directly to my chosen charities that I will discuss in the next few pages.

Day 7

Last but not least, a very efficient and very appropriate place to bring up Help a Kid in Love is in your religious setting. The object of this book was to spread love and wisdom. I can't think of another place that has such a similar objective as your place of worship. I continually have to remind myself that there are many different kinds of religions in the world, so I have to refrain from saying "church." Many people go to different places to try to heighten the amount of love and wisdom in their life. Most of the people I know go to church, but others may attend synagogues, some might live in mosques, and many of my college friends huddle around the TV once a week to worship Monday Night Football. (We won't hold that against them.)

Special Ways to Help

Although I already covered all the easy and efficient ways to help me, there are a few other areas where I could use your help if you have the skills and connections to do so. These are huge favors to ask of you, and I would be forever indebted to you if you helped in theses areas. But in order for me to tell the *entire* world, I need help translating my book and website into other languages and will need to get forms of mass media to help with my mission.

Can you write in another language? Are you good with words? Would you like to stamp your name on something that just might make history? If you are capable of translating this book and my webpage into another language, I would greatly appreciate your help and will find a way to benefit you from your efforts. On my main website there is a link that allows you to get more information on helping me with translations. If I find that you are able to translate effectively, I will contact you and let you translate the entire book and the webpage in other languages if you wish.

Telling the *entire* world you love someone is a very difficult task to do alone, and the best place to go for help is through mass media. If you are involved in, or connected to any television show, radio show, magazine, or newspaper, and if anything from my book would be beneficial to your viewers, listeners, or readers please feel free to include what you wish, and I'd be more than willing to talk to you and your audience in person for helping me tell so many people.

Contact: **chris@helpakidinlove.com**

Helping Other Kids in Love

The majority of the would-be profits from the purchase of this book and any other products related to "Help a Kid in Love" were sent to some amazing foundations that help kids get through rough times in their life, give them someone to look up to, and helps them make their wildest dreams come true.

Big Brothers Big Sisters

www.bbbs.org

Big Brothers Big Sisters is the oldest, largest and most effective youth mentoring organization in the United States. They have been the leader in one-to-one youth service for more than a century, developing positive relationships that have a direct and lasting impact on the lives of young people. Big Brothers Big Sisters serves children, ages 6 through 18, in communities all across the country. Their mission is to help children reach their potential through professionally supported, one-to-one relationships with measurable impact.

New Hope for Kids

www.newhopeforkids.com

    Letting go of something I loved so much was the hardest thing I've ever had to go through in my life. When I stop and think about the fact that I still get the opportunity to talk to Steph as a friend whenever I wish, I can only imagine what it would be like to lose someone and having to face the facts that they are no longer physically present. This incredible organization provides support for children ages 3 to 18 who are grieving the loss of a loved one. On their website they provide an "about us" link as follows:

    New Hope for Kids specializes in blending grief facilitation and intervention for children and families and granting wishes to children with life challenging illnesses. The organization is an approved IRS 501(c)3 non-profit entity and its basic philosophy recognizes that illness and death are a part of life, and asserts that understanding and grief response is essential for one to move toward hope, healing and renewal. New Hope for Kids facilitates this process with professional counseling, support groups, special events, community education and training.

Make a Wish Foundation

www.wish.org

Since 1980, the Make-A-Wish Foundation has enriched the lives of children with life-threatening medical conditions through its wish-granting work. The Foundation's mission reflects the life-changing impact that a Make-A-Wish experience has on children, families, referral sources, donors, sponsors and entire communities.

The Make-A-Wish Foundation was founded in 1980 after a little boy named Chris Greicius realized his heartfelt wish to become a police officer. Since its humble beginnings, the organization has blossomed into a worldwide phenomenon, reaching more than 144,000 children around the world. Although it has become one of the world's most well-known charities, the Make-A-Wish Foundation has maintained the grassroots fulfillment of its mission.

A network of more than 25,000 volunteers enable the Make-A-Wish Foundation to serve children with life-threatening medical conditions. Volunteers serve as wish granters, fundraisers, special events assistants and in numerous other capacities. As the Foundation continues to mature, its mission will remain steadfast. Wish children of the past, present and future will have an opportunity to share the power of a wish.

I chose the three charities to donate the majority of the proceeds of this book as their purpose for existing are aligned with the purpose of this book. Providing hope to those who need it most, giving an example to look up to, and making dreams come true were the three most important things I walked away with from my relationship with Steph. I would like all other people in the world, especially kids, to have the chance to receive these same wonderful opportunities.

THE END

    Hopefully my way of getting through a broken heart and my attitude of praise for the one I love will help you through your own situations. Even if you are not in the position of having to let go of someone so special, I still hope that my **Hea**lthy **R**elationship **T**ips in the beginning of the book improved your relationships in your life somehow. Although they are straightforward and simple, if you always keep them in mind, your relationships (although I haven't figured out how to make them last forever) will be much better while they do last. I am no Dr. Phil (just a small town kid from the middle of nowhere) but I sincerely hope that I have helped you in some way, shape, or form, whether it was through my HeaRT's, through my method of moving on, or simply from sharing my story with you.

    Hopefully you can take something away from this book that will allow you get all the things in life you desire, most importantly happiness, which is the beginning of love. If I ever get the chance to meet you personally, I pray that you will be able to tell me that your heart is free, and you are courageously following it. When you see me, tell me that you've seized the day! And while you're at it, be sure to remind me, "Memento Mori." Very often we have the tendency to forget that some day will be our last on this earth, and we just might be living differently if we never forgot this fact.

To all the ladies who have read thus far, I hope you encompass a few of Steph's amazing qualities, above all, being yourself and enjoying every minute of life while relaxing and not worrying so much. After all, "Life is too short to be anything but happy." And to any guys who were brave enough to read a book entitled "Help a Kid in Love," I hope with all my heart, that someday you may find someone as special as Steph, and that every single day you will love her like there's no tomorrow. And to the *entire* world, when that day comes when you have to let go of something you'd trade your own life for, I pray that you will remember to look up, let go, and have faith. Let your heart lead the way. Never be afraid to *use* your love. Don't ever fight it, just keep on loving. Don't waste your time and your tears trying to hide it.

I cannot thank you enough for reading this book and helping me reach my goal of spreading love to every corner of the globe. I hope you never miss the opportunity to be consumed by the raging fire of absolute love, and I hope with all my might, that you will courageously follow your heart in all that you do.

Sincerely,

Chris Miller

A Kid in Love

Chris Miller

Acknowledgements

This book and my website could have never existed without the tremendous help and support from some very special people who mean the world to me. I would like to send a message of appreciation and thanks to all the individuals who have contributed to the success of Help a Kid in Love.

Thank You:

Steph, for being the love of my life
Mom and Dad, for always loving me
Abby, for explaining to me what love is
Adam and Jess, for being my website gurus
Carol, for providing a source for market testing
Angie, for all your help and efforts with my books
Coach Quinn, for being my coach in basketball, teacher of English, mentor in life, and editor of this book
Dr. Mary-Lou Galician, for lending me Kleenex when I needed it, and for helping me understand "realistic romance"
Marshall Widman (friend and inventor) who encouraged me from the very beginning and could see the future of Help a Kid in Love when it was just an idea in my head
Mark Victor Hansen, for providing all the information I could have asked for on how to get my book in the hands of every individual on the planet
You, the reader, for taking the time to listen to what I have to say, and for helping me tell the *entire* world who I love

Chris Miller

Last Page for Steph

I'll Always Be the Man in Love with You

I'm not the hero who will always save the day.
Don't always wear the white hat, don't always know the way.
I may not even be the dream you wanted to come true,
But I'll always be the man in love with you.

I'm not the key that opens every door.
I don't have the power to give you all you want and more,
But when you're needin' somethin' special you can hold on to,
I'll always be the man in love with you.

I never could work miracles.
There may be others who can do what I can't do,
But no one else can be as good as me at lovin' you.

So when the world won't turn the way you wish it would,
And the dreams you have don't come alive as often as they should,
Remember that there's someone there whose heart is always true.
I'll always be the man in love with you.

Remember that there's someone there whose heart is always true,
Someone there to help you make it through.
I'll always be the man in love with you.

(Lyrics compliments of George Strait© '93 Boots And Spurs Music, BMI)

www.ingramcontent.com/pod-product-compliance
Lightning Source LLC
Chambersburg PA
CBHW020753160426
43192CB00006B/324